DRACULA

Between Tradition and Modernism

D0169202

TWAYNE'S MASTERWORK STUDIES

Robert Lecker, General Editor

DRACULA

Between Tradition and Modernism

Carol A. Senf

TWAYNE PUBLISHERS
An Imprint of Simon & Schuster Macmillan
New York

PRENTICE HALL INTERNATIONAL
London Mexico City New Delhi Singapore Sydney Toronto

Twayne's Masterwork Studies No. 168

Dracula: Between Tradition and Modernism
Carol A. Senf

Twayne Publishers
An Imprint of Simon & Schuster Macmillan
1633 Broadway
New York, NY 10019

Library of Congress Cataloging-in-Publication Data

Senf, Carol A.
 Dracula : between tradition and modernism / Carol A. Senf.
  p. cm. — (Twayne's masterwork studies ; no. 168)
 Includes bibliographical references and index.
 ISBN 0-8057-7844-6 (alk. paper)
  1. Stoker, Bram, 1847–1912. Dracula. 2. Horror tales, English—History and criticism. 3. Dracula, Count (Fictitious character)
4. Vampires in literature. I. Title. II. Series.
PR6037.T617D7865   1998
823'.8—dc21   98-12892
                                        CIP

This paper meets the requirements of ANSI/NISO Z3948–1992 (Permanence of Paper).

10 9 8 7 6 5 4 3 2 1

Printed in the United States of America

Contents

Bram Stoker
Used by permission of the Hulton Getty Picture Collection Limited

Note on the References and Acknowledgments

All quotations from *Dracula* come from *The Essential Dracula: The Definitive Annotated Edition of Bram Stoker's Classic Novel,* which was prepared and edited by Leonard Wolf. There are other good paperback editions of *Dracula* that I have used in class, but this edition has the virtue of Wolf's explanatory notes. Moreover, although the text of *Dracula* has suffered fewer alterations than the texts of Stoker's other novels, Wolf's edition also has the virtue of being set from the Yale University Library's copy of the second printing of the first edition.

Every book is a collaborative effort, a melding of mind with mind, idea with idea. So many people helped me prepare this text that my recognition here doesn't begin to repay the debt that I owe. Indeed it is no exaggeration to confess that I would have been unable to complete the manuscript without the generous support of the School of Literature, Communication, and Culture at the Georgia Institute of Technology and the help of Tech's excellent interlibrary loan department. In addition, I have quite obvious debts to all the other people who have written on *Dracula* and who have contributed to my understanding of Stoker's masterpiece. I am especially grateful to Barbara Belford, whose recent biography included so much new personal material on the enigmatic Stoker and who also helped me on my quest to locate an appropriate photograph of Stoker to use for the frontispiece. In addition to thanking other members of the *Dracula* "industry," I also want to thank the students at Georgia Tech who took time away from their studies to talk about *Dracula* and the period in which it was written. Finally, I also want to thank my family—my husband Jay and sons Jeremy and Andy. All three were willing to welcome the count into our home and became almost as enthusiastic about tracking down historical references as I was.

Dracula has been in print for more than a century now, and the creature of whom Stoker wrote is much older still. This book on *Dracula*, however, is dedicated to all future readers of *Dracula* in the hope that you will see both your own face in the mirror and the face of the fascinating vampire count.

Chronology: Bram Stoker's Life and Works

1847   Abraham Stoker born 8 November to Abraham Stoker, a clerk in the Civil Service at Dublin Castle, and his wife, Charlotte Matilda Blake Thornley. The third of seven children, Bram is a sickly infant. He remains an invalid for seven years and is cared for by an uncle, William Stoker, who is associated with Dublin's Fever Hospital. Dr. Stoker writes several articles on contagious diseases and practices bleeding, a procedure that may influence Stoker's treatment of both vampirism and transfusions in *Dracula*.

1849   Stoker's brother Tom is born in August when Bram is 21 months old. During the seven-year period of his invalidism, Bram listens to his mother's stories and later weaves them into his fiction, including "The Invisible Giant," published in 1881 in *Under the Sunset*.

1854   Bram's youngest brother, George, is born on 20 July. Bram leaves his bed and walks for the first time. Throughout his life, Bram remains close to George and Thornley, two years his elder, who both become physicians. George, a specialist in throat diseases, serves as a medical officer in the Russo-Turkish Wars and the South African Wars and writes *With the Unspeakables: or Two Years' Campaigning in European and Asiatic Turkey,* which provides background material for *Dracula* and *The Lady of the Shroud*.

1857   Matrimonial Causes Act gives a legally separated wife the right to keep her earnings.

1859   Darwin publishes *The Origin of Species*.

1859–1863   Stoker attends the Rev. William Wood's preparatory school in Dublin.

1863–1872   Stoker studies mathematics and science at Trinity, graduates with honors in science in 1868, and stays on for a master's degree in pure mathematics.

1866	Stoker sees Henry Irving perform at the Theatre Royal, Dublin.
1867	Reform Bill extends franchise and doubles the English electorate.
1868	Stoker enters civil service at Dublin Castle, where his father had worked for more than 50 years.
1869	Last of the Contagious Diseases Acts (earlier acts were passed in 1864 and 1866) gives authorities the right to accuse women in garrison towns of being prostitutes and to examine them for venereal disease. Women unite to get these laws repealed.
1870	First Married Women's Property Act extends the rights of women in marriage. Josephine Butler founds the Ladies National Association to repeal the Contagious Diseases Acts.
1871	Sheridan Le Fanu publishes *Carmilla*. Stoker is so influenced by this work by a fellow Irish writer that an early version of *Dracula* features a vampire countess. Deleted from the novel, this chapter is later published as "Dracula's Guest." Stoker becomes unpaid drama critic for the Dublin *Evening Mail*. His first published work, an unsigned review, appears in November. Father retires and moves, with his wife and daughters (Matilda and Margaret), to Europe where they plan to live modestly and pay off debts.
1872	Stoker delivers address, "The Necessity for Political Honesty," at Trinity. The work, published in Dublin by James Charles & Son, is his first signed work.
1875	Stoker publishes three stories in *The Shamrock*.
1876	Massacre of Christians in Turkish Bulgaria provokes anti-Turkish campaign in Britain. Abraham Stoker dies in Naples. After his father's death, Stoker chooses to be called Bram. Stoker meets Henry Irving and goes into hysterics on hearing him recite Hood's "The Dream of Eugene Aram."
1877	Stoker resigns as drama critic to work on a book for the clerks of the Petty Sessions. Stoker later turns his experiences traveling around Ireland into material for *The Snake's Pass*.
1878	Charles Stewart Parnell becomes the official head of the Irish Home Rule Party. Stoker becomes business manager of the Lyceum Theatre for Henry Irving in October, a position he holds until 1902. On 4 December Stoker marries Florence Anne Lemon Balcombe, daughter of Lieutenant-Colonel James Balcombe and his wife, Philippa. Florence, known for her beauty, had been courted by Oscar Wilde.
1879	Stoker's first book, *The Duties of Clerks of Petty Sessions in Ireland,* is published in Dublin by J. Falconer. Recognized for years as a standard for clerks in the Irish civil service, the work

	reveals Stoker's attention to detail and research ability. His only child, a son named Irving Noel Thornley Stoker, is born 31 December.
1882	Gladstone is converted to the idea of Home Rule for Ireland. The last of eighteen Married Women's Property Bills gives women a right to their own property after marriage. A collection of Stoker's short stories, *Under the Sunset,* is published in London by Sampson Low, Marston, Searle, and Ribington and dedicated to his son. Stoker receives the Bronze Medal of the Royal Humane Society for attempting to rescue a suicide.
1884	Reform Bill extends the household franchise to the rural classes in Britain and leaves only domestic help, bachelors living with their families, and the homeless without a vote.
1885	The Labouchère Amendment criminalizes male homosexuality. Stoker lectures on the United States at London Institution.
1886	Gladstone comes into office pledged to Home Rule. His first bill for Irish Home Rule splits the Liberal Party and is defeated. Stoker begins to study law. His lecture on the United States is published in London by Sampson Low, Marston & Co. as *A Glimpse of America.*
1887	Stoker travels to America to plan Lyceum tour.
1888	London's East End is terrorized by Jack the Ripper.
1889	In December Captain William O'Shea sues for divorce from his wife Katharine and names Parnell as corespondent. *The Snake's Pass,* based on Stoker's experiences as Inspector of Petty Sessions, is serialized in *People.*
1890	O'Shea wins his case. Although Parnell marries Kitty O'Shea, he never regains his political reputation. 30 April, Stoker is called to the bar. Although he never practices law, Stoker uses the law and lawyers in numerous novels. *The Snake's Pass* is published in London by Sampson Low, Marston & Co. Stoker begins work on *Dracula.*
1891	Parnell dies.
1892	Wilde's *Salome* is banned by the Lord Chamberlain's office. Stoker hears Tennyson read his poetry on a recorded cylinder, a technological device that he uses in *Dracula.* Stoker sketches a plot for *Dracula* and places events in the next year.
1893	Gladstone's second Home Rule Bill is rejected by the House of Lords.
1894	*The Watter's Mou'* is published in Westminster by Archibald Constable.
1895	*The Shoulder of Shasta* is published in Westminster by Archibald Constable. 25 May, Henry Irving and Thornley Stoker are knighted by Queen Victoria. On the same day, Oscar Wilde's

	second trial on charges of gross indecency ends with a conviction.
1897	*Dracula* is published in Westminster by Archibald Constable. On 26 May, a dramatic version is acted at the Lyceum to establish copyright and protect the drama from piracy.
1898	Stoker's only historical novel, *Miss Betty*, is published in London by C. Arthur Pearson Ltd. and dramatized 31 January.
1899	A collection of short stories, *Snowbound: The Record of a Theatrical Touring Party*, is published in London by Collier.
1900	Oscar Wilde dies 30 November. Irving signs the Lyceum over to syndicate.
1901	Death of Victoria; accession of Edward VII. Charlotte Stoker dies.
1902	*The Mystery of the Sea* is published in London by William Heinemann, and a dramatic version is presented at the Lyceum on 17 March. On 19 July, the Lyceum closes its doors.
1903	*The Jewel of Seven Stars* is published in London by William Heinemann.
1904	Irving's company embarks on its last tour of the United States.
1905	*The Man* is published in London by William Heinemann. Henry Irving dies 13 October and is buried 20 October in Westminster Abbey.
1906	*Personal Reminiscences of Henry Irving* is published in London by William Heinemann. Stoker suffers first stroke.
1908	*Lady Athlyne* is published in London by William Heinemann.
1909	*The Lady of the Shroud* is published in London by William Heinemann.
1910	Stoker suffers a second stroke. *Famous Impostors* is published in London by Sidgwick and Jackson.
1911	In February Stoker petitions the Royal Literary Fund for a grant and receives £100. Thornley Stoker is made a baronet. Stoker's last novel, *The Lair of the White Worm*, is published in London by William Rider and Son, Ltd. Stoker begins to organize three collections of published work.
1912	15 April, *Titanic* sinks on its maiden voyage. 20 April, Stoker dies with Florence and Noel at his bedside.
1914	Florence Stoker edits the stories her husband was preparing when he died and includes a previously unpublished story, "Dracula's Guest." The collection, *Dracula's Guest—And Other Weird Stories*, is published in London by George Routledge & Sons, Ltd.
1922	Florence Stoker learns of a German silent film adaptation of *Dracula* called *Nosferatu* and asks for £5,000 in royalties and

the destruction of all copies of the film. Prana, the company that produced the film, is on the verge of bankruptcy.

1924   Prana's bankruptcy case goes to court in May and is followed by 14 months of appeals. Afterward, a German court orders all copies of *Nosferatu* destroyed.

1937   25 May, Florence Stoker dies.

.

LITERARY AND HISTORICAL CONTEXT

1

Historical Context

Although the fin de siècle period (a term adopted in Britain around 1890 to describe the unique character of the end of the century) during which Bram Stoker wrote *Dracula* was a time of unprecedented and dramatic change that impacted almost every aspect of human life, Stoker himself was a product of a much more traditional world. Born in 1847 (a time described as Victorian noon or the Age of Equipoise by some historians) into a family that was conservative, Tory, and steeped in Anglo-Irish tradition, Stoker was thoroughly grounded in that traditional world. His father, who was 46 when Bram was born, had served as a civil servant in Dublin under George III, George IV, William IV, and Victoria. These turbulent years in Irish history witnessed Catholic emancipation, the Reform Acts of 1832 and 1867, the Tithe War, Protestant Repeal, several years of famine, as well as revolutions throughout the rest of Europe. Indeed, the period during which Stoker and his father lived was the time in which Ireland and the rest of Europe made the transition from a traditional world to a modern one. Stoker's life thus began at Victorian noon and ended when Europe was recognizably modern. As a result, Bram Stoker was familiar with both. He initially followed in his father's footsteps by entering the Irish civil service at Dublin Castle after graduating from Trinity College, Dublin, although he ultimately left family and traditions for a more Bohemian existence in London. As business manager to Henry Irving's Lyceum Theatre, Stoker rubbed elbows with the literary avant-garde, the political leaders of his day, and scientists and explorers. Not surprisingly then, his short stories and novels, including *Dracula*, often incorporate elements of both traditional life and avant-garde thinking, a characteristic of much fin de siècle thought.

When *Dracula* was published in 1897, people were looking forward rather than backward. Indeed, the very term "fin de siècle" usually means modern, progressive, or advanced (although some people use the term to mean decadent). This belief in progress was intensified by scientific discoveries and technological innovation. Hundreds of new inventions, such as faster railroad locomotives, oceangoing steamships, photography, phonographs, improvements in sanitation, the opening of the London Underground, and electric lighting brought improvements in day-to-day life to most Londoners. Moreover, the rapid growth of pure science transformed the nineteenth-century view of the world so dramatically that many late Victorians referred to their age as modern. Trained in mathematics and science, Bram Stoker was particularly suited to write about these developments.

Some people, however, mourned the passing of the old order, especially the losses connected with the questioning of traditional authority in religion, morality, society, even education and family life, and regarded as dangerous the experimental behaviors encouraged by the new belief in science.

Among the changes perceived as most threatening were those that involved the redefinition of sexual relationships. The earlier Victorian period had celebrated the idea of Separate Spheres for men and women and had regarded gender roles as both fixed and rigid. Thinkers at the end of the century often challenged such rigid gender roles. Furthermore, a variety of social and legal changes earlier in the century had eroded some of the traditional distinctions between men and women. Efforts to gain equal rights for women had begun as early as 1792 with Mary Wollstonecraft's *A Vindication of the Rights of Woman*. By midcentury, the movement to gain rights for women escalated, and Parliamentary debates on various issues including suffrage for women, easier access to divorce, and the rights of married women to their own property (Married Women's Property Acts) firmly placed these issues before the public eye.

By the end of the century, many people associated these demands for sexual equality with the New Woman, a phrase that characterized both a group of novelists in the 1880s and 1890s and people who desired to change the condition of women. Those individuals who were collectively considered New Women were certainly not unified in their goals for women. Nonetheless, they all wished for women to move away from traditional roles as wives and mothers. The New Woman was a controversial figure, aiming at access to education and professional opportunities, free union (not marriage), and the suffrage. Frequently accused by conservative thinkers of undermining morality and religion but heralded by progressives as a force for positive changes, the New Woman gained many of these rights only after World War I. Nevertheless, these demands for changes in women's status made an impact on Stoker and his contemporaries.

Also hotly debated during this fin de siècle period was homosexuality. Indeed, conservative critics tended to see the New Woman and the homosexual man as two sides of the same decadent culture that unnaturally reversed normal gender relationships. Moreover, during the 1890s, medical theory constructed an absolute category that isolated "the homosexual" from "normal" men and women. Not surprisingly, changes in the criminal code brought the issue of homosexuality directly into public scrutiny. The Labouchère Amendment of 1885 criminalized male homosexuality for the first time in history, and the publicity surrounding the Oscar Wilde trials made the public even more aware of the issue. Wilde, formerly a friend of the Stokers and a fellow Irishman, became a social pariah after his conviction in 1895 for gross indecency. Medical theory and social policy succeeded in branding the effeminate male as a type of monstrous aberration.

While discussions of changing gender relations at home alternately thrilled and frightened Stoker and his contemporaries, the acquisition of additional territory and power across the globe also raised new social and political issues. During the nineteenth century, England acquired new territory from Canada to India and became the empire on which the sun never set. By the end of the nineteenth century, the British Empire directly controlled one-quarter of the earth's land surface and was the greatest economic power in the world. Despite scattered colonial opposition (the bloody Indian Mutiny of 1857, the Jamaica Rebellion of 1865, territorial unrest in Africa, and the seemingly endless difficulties with Ireland), the relative stability of the empire suggested that it would endure indefinitely.

The seeds of its demise were beginning to take root, however. Not only did the debate over Home Rule for Ireland raise issues regarding colonial autonomy throughout the empire, but many people debated the relationship of England to the indigenous people in all the colonies. Although British imperialism depended on confidence in Britain's economic and political future, it also relied on paternalist and racist theory that regarded the governing of colonial subjects as a duty, as in Rudyard Kipling's well-known phrase, "the white man's burden." In effect, the empire provided a convincing argument of the Social Darwinists' conviction that, fittest of all nations, England deserved to dominate others. Some thinkers worried about the moral influence that these conquered peoples would have on England, however, even arguing that the relationship with such primitive people would ultimately destroy England itself.

Swirling with changes in almost all areas, the fin de siècle time was an exciting period in which to live and write, a period in which grand social, economic, political, and aesthetic questions were being hotly debated. As fervently as the Modernists challenged existing ideas, traditionalists defended them. Thus, Janus-like, the final decades of the century looked in two opposing directions. Vestiges of High Victorianism and traditional thinking remained strong, and many people looked nostalgically to the past, a period that they believed contained a clear synthesis of moral, religious, artistic, political, and social thought. On the other hand, rising Modernism challenged people to rethink these traditional values and to come to terms with a more scientific, experimental world. Bram Stoker grappled with these issues and, like the period in which he lived, anticipated the future but could not break away entirely from the past.

2

The Importance of the Work

Dracula is important for its influence on literature, film, and popular culture in general. The sheer number of works with "Dracula" in their title tempts me to argue that no other single work, with the exception of the Bible, has so influenced Anglo-American culture. Hardly a school child in Europe or North America would fail to recognize the vampire count (although that child is certainly more likely to know Dracula from a film or comic book interpretation than from Stoker's novel).

Moreover, *Dracula* revolutionized twentieth-century ideas about vampires. Whereas Coleridge, Polidori, and Le Fanu transformed a folklore belief into a literary icon, Stoker emphasized the multiple natures of the vampire and also placed the vampire squarely in the modern world. Furthermore, he was the first writer to use the vampire to suggest the intersection of myth and science, past and present.

Understanding *Dracula* also provides insights into Stoker's times, including insights about changing standards of sexual behavior, the broader roles allotted to women, the place of England in the world, and the impact of science and technology on that world. Indeed, *Dracula* is a veritable mirror of fin de siècle beliefs. Because of his family background, personal and professional relationships, and interests, Stoker was ideally placed to comment on this period, which simultaneously looked back nostalgically to a stable, traditional world and forward enthusiastically to the modern one.

Although Stoker cannot be considered part of the group described as the aesthetes or decadents, he was personally acquainted with Oscar Wilde, whom he met in the 1870s when Stoker was a student at Trinity College. While living in Dublin, Stoker became friends with Wilde's parents. He even used Egyptian archaeological material in *The Jewel of Seven Stars* that he could have learned from Sir William Wilde. (Wilde traveled in Egypt as private physician to a wealthy patient and learned about both eye diseases and ancient monuments.) Stoker and his family continued to visit Lady Wilde when she moved to London in 1876 after her husband's death. Stoker and Oscar Wilde were linked even more closely by the fact that both courted Florence Balcombe; Wilde maintained ties with Florence after she married Stoker and both families settled in London. In addition to sending flowers and notes to Florence, Wilde continued to send copies of his works, including *The Happy Prince and Other Tales* and a copy of the first French edition of *Salome*. That Stoker was not more supportive when Wilde was convicted and imprisoned for homosexuality in 1895 is therefore surprising. Stoker's friends Ellen Terry and Henry Irving actively supported Wilde, and Stoker even received an appeal for help from Oscar's brother, Willie. Stoker was working on *Dracula* during the Wilde trials, and it is difficult not to see that the gender relationships in the novel were influenced by Wilde's behavior and by the anger of his detractors. It is more difficult to determine Stoker's feelings on these issues.

Dracula may be important because of the light it sheds on nineteenth-century notions of homosexuality, but Stoker was undoubtedly thinking about the New Woman while he wrote it. Lucy Westenra and the three vampire-women in Dracula's castle share traits that Stoker and his contemporaries associated with the New Woman: All four are sexual predators who relate to children as objects to devour rather than to protect, and all four initiate sexual relationships rather than wait patiently for men.

Lest readers miss the connection between female vampires and the New Woman, Stoker made the direct connection at the beginning of chapter 8 when Mina Harker criticizes the New Woman. Mina writes in her journal that she and Lucy had dined in an old-fashioned inn and that they would have shocked the "New Woman" with their appetites. Later Mina examines courtship rituals, saying that Lucy's fiancé, who fell in love with her in the drawing room, would love her more if he saw her in her bedroom. Mina adds sarcastically: "But I suppose the New Woman won't condescend in future to accept; she will do the proposing herself." Such critical commentary seems to set Mina, whose courtship and subsequent marriage follow traditional patterns, apart from the typical New Woman. Indeed, Mina seems to desire nothing more than to help her husband advance in his career. She also nurtures all the men in the novel, cradling the sorrowing Arthur Holmwood in her arms and comparing him to "the baby that some day may lie on my bosom." Unlike the other female characters, Mina is celebrated at the conclusion of the novel as a mother with a child at her side, the epitome of traditional womanhood.

Other actions by Mina, however, including her participation in the quest to destroy Dracula, seem to ally her with the more independent New Woman. Her character thus reflects the tensions of the times regarding changing roles for women. As a result, the question about Stoker's attitude toward the New Woman is difficult to answer, as can be attested by the quantity of debate on this subject by contemporary feminists.

Dracula also provides insights into late nineteenth-century imperialism. Not only did Stoker come from a family of civil servants (three generations of Stokers at Dublin Castle represented English interests in Ireland and regulated the lives of both the ruling Anglo-Irish and the indigenous Irish), but Stoker himself served 10 years as a civil servant at Dublin Castle and titled his first book *The Duties of Clerks of Petty Sessions in Ireland* (1878). Two brothers were civil servants, Richard in the Indian Medical Service and Tom in the foreign service. In addition, after settling in London, Stoker became friends with William Ewert Gladstone, the Liberal prime minister whose name was synonymous with Home Rule for Ireland and who often sought Stoker's opinion on Irish matters. A self-proclaimed "philosophical

Home-Ruler," Stoker was quiet about this belief because Irving mocked him about it. Nevertheless, most of Stoker's novels, including *Dracula*, address the relationships of the English with various native peoples and the question of converting those peoples to the English way of life. Various critics (including Stephen D. Arata, Joseph Bristow, and Judith Halberstam) have examined Stoker's interest in imperialism, although more work remains to be done on this topic.

Connected to Stoker's interest in imperialism and his concern that the moral values of Europe were being eroded from within and from without was his interest in science and technology and their impact on his world. Most definitely, *Dracula* reveals Stoker's fascination with the technological developments of his own time—the telegraphs, the typewriters, the phonographs, and the Winchester rifles that his heroes use in their fight against the vampire count. That Stoker came from a family interested in science (an uncle and two brothers were physicians; and Stoker earned a baccalaureate degree in science, a master's in mathematics, and a degree in law) and that he used modern science and technology in *Dracula* seems to argue for his celebration of science.

On the other hand, although the principal figures in *Dracula* believe in technology and professional training, they also rely on very traditional weapons in their battle with the vampire, including crucifixes, wooden stakes, garlic, and the Host. The conclusion remains open-ended because Dracula, who is stabbed by Harker's knife rather than staked as protocol seems to demand, may simply have vanished into mist instead of being destroyed. Thus, the novel encourages readers to go beyond the uncritical views of Stoker's characters and to examine our relationship to science and technology just as it encourages readers to examine views on race and gender.

In conclusion, *Dracula* deserves our attention not only because of what it reveals about the times in which it was written but also because it encourages us to reexamine the views of our own day. Certainly the key to the importance of *Dracula* rests in its popularity, a popularity that continues undiminished a century after its initial publication. *Dracula* continues to fascinate us because it both reveals the contradictions of Stoker's own day and points us to the internal tensions of our own.

3

Critical Reception

Stoker was well known in London literary and artistic circles because he served as business manager for the Lyceum Theatre for 24 years, a position that put him in touch with the intellectual leaders of his time. He was also a prolific writer, although of his 18 books (novels, romances, and nonfiction), *Dracula* is the only work that continues to elicit either scholarly or critical attention. In fact, even in its own day *Dracula* was better reviewed than anything else that Stoker wrote.[1]

Stoker's own views about his most famous novel are elusive. One biographer, Barbara Belford, observes that Stoker spent more than six years working on *Dracula*, a significant amount of time considering his busy professional schedule and the fact that he completed other novels in as few as three weeks. She indicates that Stoker made the first notes for the novel that eventually became *Dracula* on 8 March 1890 and that the last date recorded is 17 March 1896. Belford explains that Stoker had sketched out a plot by February 1892 and had placed events in the next calendar year. She also notes that he originally planned to kill Dracula on his birthday, 8 November, but that the final draft of the novel concludes two days earlier.[2] Belford argues that, because of Stoker's careful attention to details, *Dracula* reveals a great deal about the man who wrote it; other critics have used the novel to learn about its notedly reticent writer. David Glover, author of the first scholarly study of Stoker's fiction, is quick to argue a different case: Although Stoker "invites a biographical reading by playfully scattering topical references and allusions throughout his work," provides "elements of self-portraiture in several of his heroes," and bases the places and people in his novels on "those he knew well," these autobiographical materials do not mean that *Dracula* can be read as an "elaborate roman à clef."[3] Glover's attitude is sensible, and like Glover, I believe it is important to read the novel on its own merits rather than to speculate on questions that will never be answered.

One of the first people to provide a contemporary response to *Dracula* was Stoker's mother. Charlotte Stoker compared the novel to *Frankenstein* and thereby connected two of the great science-gothics of the nineteenth century, a connection that continues to exist: "No book since Mrs. Shelley's 'Frankenstein' or indeed any other at all has come near yours in originality, or terror—Poe is nowhere." Literary acquaintances—including sensation writer Mary Elizabeth Braddon, adventure writer Anthony Hope Hawkins, and detective novelist Arthur Conan Doyle—were equally enthusiastic. Braddon, best known for *Lady Audley's Secret*, had in the previous year written a vampire tale of her own involving a physician-hero and a young woman whose blood is used to keep an aged crone alive. Despite the similarities in plot, Braddon found *Dracula* vastly superior to her own "Good Lady Ducayne." She wrote to Stoker on 23 June 1897 to congratulate him on *Dracula*: "We will talk of it more anon! when I have soberly read and meditated thereupon. I have done my humdrum little story of transfusion ... but your 'bloofer lady' ..." Hawkins wrote to complain that Stoker's vampires had robbed him of sleep.[4]

Dracula was well received by contemporary reviewers, who also commented on Stoker's ability to frighten his audience. The *Spectator* reviewer, for example, praised Stoker for his ability to "eclipse all previous efforts in the domain of the horrible," to improve on the efforts of Wilkie Collins, Sheridan Le Fanu, and other practitioners of "the flesh-creeping school."[5] In addition, the reviewer for the *Bookman* warned readers to keep the novel away from "nervous children," though he added that adult readers "will both shudder and enjoy" the events in the novel.[6]

More critical was the reviewer for the *Atheneum*, who objected to both the plot and the characterization and who described *Dracula* as "a mere series of grotesquely incredible events," adding, however, that some sections of the novel "show more power." The reviewer wrote that Stoker sometimes "almost succeeds in creating the sense of possibility in impossibility; at others he merely commands an array of crude statements of incredible actions." Finally, the reviewer criticized the weakness of the characters, an observation that readers and scholars today continue to make.[7]

The reviewer for the *Spectator* also commended Stoker's myth-making ability, but objected to the "up-to-dateness of the book."[8] In fact, the reviewer noted that all the technological material "hardly fits in with the mediaeval methods which ultimately secure the victory for Count Dracula's foes." Indeed, Stoker's exploration of topical materials, including science and technology, is much more likely to be admired by twentieth-century critics than it was by Stoker's contemporaries.[9]

Contemporary reviews, although they recognized that *Dracula* was more powerful than Stoker's earlier works, were not inclined to examine why it exerted such a hold on them and were more likely to take it at face value as a horror story—as did the *Punch* reviewer who compared the novel to *Faust*.[10]

Although the critics' response has been mixed since the novel was first published, *Dracula* has always been immensely popular with ordinary readers. In fact, it has never been out of print in English, and it has been translated into numerous foreign languages. In addition, the novel has been a favorite for both dramatic and film interpretations, including F. W. Murnau's *Nosferatu, the Vampire* (1922); Tod Browning's *Dracula*, starring Bela Lugosi (1931); and literally hundreds of others that are loosely based on the novel.[11] However, like the novel, these films have been regarded as popular and have received relatively little critical or scholarly attention until recently. Between 1897 and 1972, only three works focused on *Dracula*, one of them Harry Ludlam's 1962 biography, *A Biography of Dracula: The*

Life Story of Bram Stoker.[12] The others are Bacil F. Kirtley, "Dracula, the Monastic Chronicles and Slavic Folk-lore,"[13] and Richard Wasson, "The Politics of *Dracula.*"[14]

The year 1972 witnessed a veritable rebirth of scholarly interest in *Dracula.* Charles Osborne edited *The Bram Stoker Bedside Companion,*[15] which made "Dracula's Guest" (the original first chapter of *Dracula*) and numerous other Stoker short stories available to readers for the first time in more than 50 years. Raymond T. MacNally and Radu Florescu's *In Search of Dracula*[16] and Leonard Wolf's *A Dream of Dracula*[17] examined Stoker's life as well as the life of Vlad V of Romania, the historical figure on which Stoker based Dracula. In "The Monster in the Bedroom: Sexual Symbolism in Bram Stoker's *Dracula,*"[18] Christopher Bentley applied psychoanalytic techniques to Stoker's novel while Joseph S. Bierman, in *"Dracula*: Prolonged Childhood Illness and the Oral Triad," applied the tools of psychoanalysis to Stoker himself.[19] Ernest Fontana, in "Lombroso's Criminal Man and Stoker's *Dracula,*" looked at *Dracula* within the context of late-nineteenth-century thought. Jean Gattegno, in "Folie, Croyance et Fantastique dans 'Dracula',"[20] and Royce MacGillivray, in " 'Dracula': Bram Stoker's Spoiled Masterpiece,"[21] examined the literary merits and defects of Stoker's novel. In fact, MacGillivray claimed that only Stoker's weak characterization prevented *Dracula* from being recognized as a masterpiece.

Today, more than a quarter century after that rebirth of interest in Dracula, scholars and critics continue to fine-tune the critical strategies of these early scholars. Despite the existence of three biographies (Harry Ludlam, Barbara Belford, and Daniel Farson)[22] and other short biographical studies, Stoker remains an enigma. Psychological studies of Stoker are likely to continue. Psychoanalytic studies include Phyllis A. Roth's full-length study of Stoker[23] and the study by Clive Leatherdale, who summarizes the psychoanalytical approach as well as several other approaches in *Dracula: The Novel and the Legend.*[24]

Scholars also continue to be interested in the relationship between *Dracula* and the times that produced it and in the connection between *Dracula* and various literary genres and strategies. Among the best of the studies that examine Stoker's relationship to the times in which he lived are Stephen D. Arata's look at *Dracula* as a novel that examines British anxiety about being colonized;[25] Patrick Brantlinger's look at Dracula as an example of British fears of atavism;[26] and Burton Hatlen's Marxist study of *Dracula* as the fear of the "other."[27]

Continuing in the direction first reopened by MacGillivray, other scholars are examining the literary merits of *Dracula*. Among the more interesting literary studies are those by Alison Case and Ronald D. Morrison, which focus on the novel's complex narrative structure.[28]

While *Dracula* continues to lend itself to the efforts of psychological scholarship, historical scholarship, and genre studies, it has also yielded itself to other critical approaches, including feminist studies, queer theory, cultural studies, and science studies.

Feminist scholars, including Stephanie Demetrakopoulos, Gail B. Griffin, and Cyndy Hendershot, have found Stoker's treatment of women characters to be a veritable gold mine of material about gender and the relationships between the sexes.[29] Queer theorists, including Christopher Craft and Talia Schaffer, have been fascinated by Stoker's handling of gender issues and by his relationship to Oscar Wilde, whose notorious trial was going on while Stoker was writing the novel.[30] John Greenway, Rosemary Jann, Jennifer Wicke, and other scholars of science and technology have been fascinated by Stoker's examination of these fields and by the fact that the novel focuses on the conflict between Dracula, a Renaissance warlord, and residents of turn-of-the-century London.[31]

The novel continues to attract attention from literary critics, students of popular culture, and film critics. In fact, recent criticism explores how the novel touches on anxieties about the British imperial presence as well as on anxieties about gender relationships and questions of identity and how these complex issues are intertwined in nineteenth-century ideology. David Glover's *Vampires, Mummies, and Liberals: Bram Stoker and the Politics of Popular Fiction* is the first full study of Stoker as a popular writer and the first to take Stoker seriously as a writer whose experiments in fantasy are deliberate attempts to communicate with his audience. Glover, who takes a cultural studies approach to Stoker's writings, sees Stoker very much as a man of his times and examines the ways in which all his novels engage the moral, scientific, and political thought of their day. As such, Glover's study is likely to open up an entirely new dimension in the discussion of *Dracula* and of Stoker's other fiction. Given the continued popularity of *Dracula* with ordinary readers and its relatively recent discovery by the scholarly community, one might even venture to guess that as new critical methodologies evolve, their practitioners will continue to find that *Dracula* is a rich and provocative text.

A READING

4

Narrative Strategy in *Dracula*: Journals, Newspapers, and Diaries

Readers familiar with any of the numerous film versions of *Dracula* will already know the basic plot line of the novel in which a small group of heroic individuals bands together to rid the world of the monstrous vampire that threatens to destroy all human life. None of these film versions, however, has managed to capture either the symmetry or the complexity of Stoker's narration.

Although Stoker divides *Dracula* into chapters rather than into parts, the novel is easier to understand in terms of its four distinct parts, or sections. The first of these parts relates Jonathan Harker's trip to Dracula's castle, when an ordinary business trip becomes a terrifying encounter with four powerful supernatural creatures. In the second part, Dracula comes to England, where he seduces and destroys an innocent English girl, Lucy Westenra. This part, which is also a kind of medical mystery in which two physicians attempt to understand what is happening to their patient, ends with Lucy's being destroyed by Dr. Van Helsing and three young men who had proposed marriage to her. The third section brings together a number of characters to battle Dracula and includes the seduction of Mina Harker and the decision to track Dracula to his castle. The fourth section includes the chase, in which this unified group tracks Dracula to his castle and finally destroys him. Dividing the novel into sections also helps readers to observe the symmetry in the novel: There are two journeys to Transylvania, because the group at the conclusion follows much the same path that Jonathan Harker followed at the beginning; and there are two women who come into contact with Dracula although the results of their encounters with the vampire are markedly different.

Although first-time readers may miss the symmetry of the novel, they are likely to notice its unique narrative strategy. In fact, few other novels unite the extreme subjectivity of the eighteenth-century epistolary novel with the objectivity of journalistic accounts. Whereas other Victorian novelists were likely to employ either a first-person narration (such as a diary, memoir, or other method of self-revelation) or a third-person narration that enables the novelist to examine the thoughts of numerous characters, Stoker chose to tell his story of a powerful supernatural figure through an assortment of ordinary documents, including letters, diary and journal entries, and newspaper clippings. It is a strategy that privileges the reader, who, acting like a detective to piece together the information that the characters present, is likely to solve the mysteries before the characters do. Furthermore, it is a strategy that unites the uncanny with the ordinary, the ancient with the modern, and the mythic with the scientific.

Although *Dracula* is told through the "voices" of numerous narrators from a number of countries who speak a variety of dialects, Stoker chooses to tell most of the story through the written accounts of four main narrators: Jonathan Harker, a young solicitor, goes to Transylvania to do business with Count Dracula and keeps a journal of what happens as he travels across Europe and later when he is imprisoned in Dracula's castle; Harker's wife, Mina née Murray, writes letters to her childhood friend Lucy Westenra and starts a journal both to practice her shorthand and to emulate lady journalists; Lucy Westenra, Dracula's first English victim, writes letters and keeps a journal to imitate her friend Mina; and Dr. John Seward, the director of a London mental asylum, records the case histories of his patients and his personal diary on a phonograph. The personal accounts of these four individuals constitute roughly 80 percent of *Dracula*.

I discuss the significance of these four major narrators later in this chapter, but it is important to point out that Stoker includes two categories of additional narrators: narrators who are also major actors in the plot and narrators who are important because they provide information that the main characters would be unlikely to know.

Among the major characters in the novel who occasionally serve as narrators are Arthur Holmwood, Quincey Morris, and Dr. Van Helsing. Holmwood, later Lord Godalming, is the fiancé of Lucy Westenra as well as the individual who provides most of the financial backing for the fight against Dracula. Aside from Count Dracula, Holmwood is also the only aristocrat in the novel. His only contributions to the narrative are a telegram to Quincey Morris,[1] a letter to Dr. Seward (144), and a telegram, also to Dr. Seward (145). None of these written communications does much more than reveal that he is a faithful friend, a loving fiancé, and a devoted son.

Quincey P. Morris, an American from Texas, (for further discussion of the significance of Morris's American background, see the next chapter) is also part of the group that follows Dracula to Transylvania and destroys him. Although Morris loses his own life in the process, he contributes even less to the narration than his friend Holmwood, for his single contribution is a letter to Arthur Holmwood (81–82).

Because Holmwood, Morris, and Seward are portrayed as old friends who once shared adventures and who even now share a similar perspective on life, it is perhaps logical that Stoker does not attempt to divide the narration among such similar characters. It is somewhat more strange that he allots so little of the narration to Dr. Abraham Van Helsing, who is often described as the leader of the small group that fights against Dracula and is sometimes described as the novel's father figure and the voice of Stoker himself, a connection suggested because he and Stoker share the patriarchal name of Abraham. Nonetheless, although Van Helsing provides both readers and his fellow characters with most of the background mythology about vampires, he contributes surprisingly little to the actual written record:

several letters, notes, and memoranda to Dr. Seward, his old pupil; several telegrams; and a little other correspondence. Van Helsing's portion of the narration is important in that his letter to Mina Harker unites the entire group in its quest against Dracula. Moreover, his memorandum at the conclusion reveals the power that the vampire wields over even knowledgeable people. Unlike Jonathan Harker, who had briefly almost succumbed to the seductive power of the three vampire-women at Dracula's castle, Van Helsing knows precisely the danger of these temptresses. That he nonetheless almost succumbs to them is proof of the vampire's power over ordinary human beings: "She was so fair to look on, so radiantly beautiful, so exquisitely voluptuous, that the very instinct of man in me, which calls some of my sex to love and to protect one of hers, made my head whirl with new emotion" (437). Although Van Helsing will steel himself to destroy the three vampire-women, his memorandum allows the reader to see exactly how tempting they are.

Stoker also includes the accounts of individuals who are not characters in the novel but who provide important information about Dracula that readers and characters could not otherwise know. Included are several cuttings from newspapers. The first, a cutting from *The Dailygraph* pasted in Mina's journal, tells of the Russian ship the *Demeter* and its mysterious arrival in Whitby. Although the characters do not yet know of Dracula's presence in England, readers will already suspect that Dracula is responsible for the deaths of the crew members. Moreover, the newspaper account and the excerpt from the captain's log reinforce that ordinary people are poorly prepared for their encounter with the vampire.

A second newspaper clipping, this time from *The Pall Mall Gazette*, tells about the escaped wolf Bersicker, whom the reader later discovers is Dracula's entry to Lucy Westenra's home. This humorous account reveals once more Dracula's power over the animal world.

A third newspaper account, from *The Westminster Gazette*, reports that a "bloofer lady" has been playing with children around Hamstead Heath and has left tiny bite marks on their necks. Remembering the tendency of the vampire-women to prey on children, readers will suspect Lucy Westenra of being this beautiful predator even before Van Helsing reveals to Seward, Holmwood, and Morris that Lucy has become a vampire.

In addition to the three newspaper accounts, the novel includes a report from Dr. Seward's associate Dr. Patrick Hennessey on the condition of Renfield, one of Seward's patients, and several letters that provide additional information about Dracula's whereabouts and business affairs. Salli Kline[2] objects to these letters and argues that they could not have come into the possession of Stoker's primary narrators. She cites as particular evidence of Stoker's carelessness correspondence between Samuel F. Billington & Son, Solicitors, Whitby, and Messrs. Carter, Paterson & Co., London, on 17 and 21 August and the note Van Helsing leaves in his portmanteau, Berkeley Hotel, directed to John Seward, M.D., but not delivered.[3] Kline finds little good to say of *Dracula* and concludes her study of the novel by describing it as "an incendiary, demagogic work of literature containing pre-fascist fantasies of annihilating 'degenerate' human beings and their 'degenerate' artistic products" that deserves attention only for what it reveals about the times in which it was written.[4]

Although it is true that Stoker is occasionally careless about details and that *Dracula* deserves attention for what it reveals about the times in which it was written, it is equally true that *Dracula* has other literary merits. The remainder of this chapter demonstrates that Stoker's narrative strategy is much more sophisticated than Kline or most other commentators have suggested.

Certainly, the four main narrators reinforce ideas and attitudes that are merely suggested by some of the minor narrators. The result is ultimately a remarkable union of sentiment among the primary group of individuals who, in joining the battle against Dracula, lose much of their uniqueness as individuals and become representatives of all England—possibly of all Western Europe—in the battle against the evil that they perceive in the vampire.

The first of these main narrators, Jonathan Harker, is the novel's single narrative voice for the first 69 pages. Formerly a solicitor's clerk, he has recently become a full solicitor, and he will ultimately inherit the firm from his employer and surrogate father, Peter Hawkins. A representative of the British legal system, he is a spokesman for the value of English law as well as for nineteenth-century progress and morality. Indeed, the mere fact that his diary is in shorthand—"nineteenth century up-to-date with a vengeance" (49–50) identifies him as modern as do his comments on inefficient travel as he moves further away from civilized London. He notes initially that his impression of Buda-Pesth was of "leaving the West and entering the East" (1) and adds that "the further East you go the more unpunctual are the trains. What ought they to be in China?" (5). Thus, even before he comes to Dracula's castle, Harker's journal privileges the West over the East, the present over the past, and reason, progress, and modernity over superstition, nostalgia, and primitiveness. Indeed, Harker repeatedly identifies the region through which he travels as primitive and strange, a place where "every known superstition in the world is gathered" (4) and where the natives are strange, even barbarian.

Surrounded in his travels by unfamiliar behavior and strange customs that he cannot understand, Harker ultimately finds himself in a setting that seems to exemplify that primitive past, "a vast ruined castle, from whose tall black windows came no ray of light, and whose broken battlements showed a jagged line against the moonlit sky" (19). Even more disconcerting, however, is the owner of that castle, for Dracula identifies himself as leader of these barbarians and also reminds Harker that "Transylvania is not England. Our ways are not your ways, and there shall be to you many strange things" (29).

Most strange to Harker is Dracula's identification with the past. More like a Renaissance warlord than a resident of modern Europe, Dracula is comfortable with the wolves and with his memories of the warlike past: "The warlike days are over. Blood is too precious a thing in these days of dishonourable peace; and the glories of the great races are as a tale that is told" (42). Such behavior makes Harker uneasy even before he begins to suspect that Dracula is a different order of being: "What manner of man is this, or what manner of creature is it in the semblance of man?" (48). Devoted proponent of progress that he is, Harker will ultimately come to fear that "the old centuries had, and have, powers of their own which mere 'modernity' cannot kill" (50), and the question of the power of the past is one that *Dracula* poses throughout. Harker also worries that he is responsible for transporting this monster from the past to London, where "perhaps, for centuries to come he might, amongst its teeming millions, satiate his lust for blood, and create a new and ever-widening circle of semi-demons to batten on the helpless" (67).

Particularly important in Harker's narration is the fact that Stoker consistently has him think in legal terms, and Stoker's working notes for the novel suggest that he had originally planned to emphasize legal matters even more. Clive Leatherdale looks at material that originally preceded Harker's narrative:

> In fact, the relationship between "Dracula's Guest" and *Dracula* cannot be that straightforward. Stoker's papers dated 29 February 1892 reveal that the Munich events—which were scheduled to span two chapters—were themselves to be preceded by an opening chapter presenting a flurry of legal correspondence relating to property sales.[5]

The novel contains somewhat less emphasis on the law although Harker should be recognized as one of a number of attorney characters created by Stoker, who was himself called to the bar on 30 April 1890, about the same time he began research on the novel that would become *Dracula*. For example, Harker is disturbed that he is a prisoner in Dracula's castle "without that protection of the law which is even a criminal's right and consolation" (60). More important in terms of the narrative is that Harker insists on facts and quickly begins to build a case based on facts: "Let me begin with facts—bare, meagre facts, verified by books and figures, and of which there can be no doubt. I must not confuse them with experiences which will have to rest on my own observation, or my memory of them" (42–43). In fact, the entire novel is in some ways an elaborate legal case against the vampire constructed largely by Harker and his wife, and he observes at roughly the novel's midpoint, "Mina and I have worked all day, and we have put all the papers into order" (276).

In addition to commenting on his strange surroundings and on the monstrous behavior of his host, Harker also indicates that he has certain beliefs about appropriate behavior for women. For example, his journal reveals a genuine fondness for his fiancée, but it also reveals that he sees her in terms of traditional gender stereotypes (chapter 6 has more on the treatment of women in *Dracula*) and that he expects his wife to be both ladylike and domestic. Initially shocked by the peasant women whose clothes are "almost too tight for modesty" (6), he is later paralyzed when he is approached by the three vampire-women at Dracula's castle. Identifying them initially as "ladies by their dress and manner" (51), he is both thrilled and horrified by their distinctly unladylike behavior when they attempt to kiss him.

Furthermore, Harker's journal introduces yet one more question that will resurface throughout the novel: the issue of sanity, which is especially important in Dr. Seward's sections of the narration. Alison Case observes that Harker's greatest fear is that his journal is a "witness against his sanity." Although his final actions in the castle may seem courageous, "they can only be seen that way within a framework of knowledge that acknowledges his judgment of his situation as accurate."[6] Thus the issue of Harker's sanity is linked directly with his own desire to provide rational evidence of what he has seen. Furthermore, although Harker does question his sanity—he is, after all, confronted with strange things that lie outside his experience—Stoker constructs the narration so that the reader is encouraged not to question Harker's sanity. Even though he and Mina are married in a hospital in Buda-Pesth where Harker is recovering from brain fever after his escape from Dracula's castle, Van Helsing examines Harker and pronounces him both sane and fit to be one of the leaders in the battle against Dracula. Harker's journal, which is interspersed throughout the remainder of the novel, continues to stress the issues found in the opening section. A note at the end, written seven years later, concludes the novel. Because this note wraps up the entire story, not just Harker's part of the narration, I discuss it after I have discussed the remaining narrators.

The second major narrator is Mina Harker, whose first letter to her friend Lucy Westenra identifies herself as an overworked assistant schoolmistress. In addition, she reveals that she is eager to help her husband with his work: "I have been practising shorthand very assiduously. When we are married I shall be able to be useful to Jonathan, and if I can stenograph well enough I can take down what he wants to say in this way and write it out for him on the typewriter, at which also I am practising very hard" (72).

As is appropriate for a wife who is eager to help her husband advance in his career, Mina often echoes the same values and beliefs as her husband. Her belief in the progress that comes with technology is evident in her shorthand and typewriting skills; her idea that women should be domestic partners echoes throughout her journal; and her belief in the power of the law is often revealed by her pride in Jonathan's legal acumen. However, Mina is not simply a feminine echo of her husband. The attention to detail found in her diary initially comes from her desire to emulate *lady* journalists "interviewing and writing descriptions and trying to remember conversations" (72) rather than from her familiarity with the law.

Mina's attention to detail enables readers to discover Dracula's presence at Whitby long before any of the characters do. In terms of the narrative strategy, Mina's attention to detail also leads her to compile all the documents surrounding Dracula's activities. Indeed she notes in her journal: "In this matter dates are everything, and I think that if we get all our material ready, and have every item put in chronological order, we shall have done much" (272). Thus she collects everything pertaining to Dracula, puts the information in chronological order, types it in multiple copies so that all the people involved can have their own copy, and distributes the copies to her husband, Van Helsing, Seward, Morris, and Holmwood. Readers should thus conclude that the novel that they see is the result of Mina's narrative strategy.

Jennifer Wicke, one of the few critics to examine *Dracula*'s unique narrative strategy, comments on Mina's importance and observes that, as the novel progresses, Mina comes to be "the author of the text" as she takes over sections of its narration. Wicke also observes that Mina is "responsible for giving her vampire-hunting colleagues all information on Dracula's whereabouts, and she is still the one who coordinates and collates the manuscripts." Wicke adds that Mina's "collation is by no means strictly secretarial, either; Mina is the one who has the idea of looking back over the assembled manuscripts for clues to Dracula's habits and his future plans."[7] In a sense then, the novel that we know as *Dracula* is largely controlled and manipulated by Mina Harker until near the conclusion. At this point, as the group approaches Dracula's castle, Mina loses control over the narration as she comes more and more under the vampire's spell.

Two more things should be noted in the sections of the novel that Mina narrates. One is her interest in money, an interest that is entirely appropriate to a young woman, apparently an orphan, who has had to support herself. She greatly appreciates Mr. Hawkins's making Jonathan his heir, and she comments frequently on the power of money: "And, too, it made me think of the wonderful power of money! What can it not do when it is properly applied; and what might it do when basely used. I felt so thankful that Lord Godalming is rich, and that both he and Mr. Morris, who also has plenty of money, are willing to spend it so freely" (420). Although the other narrators are rarely as open in their appreciation of money as Mina is, it is nonetheless evident that money is important to all of them. They frequently comment on the importance of bribery as they track Dracula back to his castle and of their ability to purchase the best, most advanced equipment.

A second characteristic of Mina's narration is her nurturing function. Whereas the three women in Dracula's castle and Lucy Westenra, once she falls under the vampire's spell, prey on others, especially children, Mina sees herself as a mother to the other characters in the novel. Meeting Arthur Holmwood for the first time, she opens her arms to him instinctively and notes:

> We women have something of the mother in us that makes us rise above smaller matters when the mother-spirit is invoked; I felt this big sorrowing man's head resting on me, as though it were that of the baby that some day may lie on my bosom, and I stroked his hair as though he were my own child. I never thought at the time how strange it all was. (278)

A page later, she tells the sorrowful Quincey Morris, "I wish I could comfort all who suffer from the heart" (279). Pictured at the conclusion with her child by her side, she is celebrated by her husband for "her sweetness and loving care" (445). Her willingness to care for others extends even to Dracula. In fact, although she recognizes him as a force of Evil, she is the only character to pity him—"I suppose one ought to pity any thing so hunted" (277)—and to comment on his death: "I shall be glad as long as I live that even in that moment of final dissolution, there was in the face a look of peace, such as I never could have imagined might have rested there" (443). This observation reveals the extent to which Mina has escaped the vampire's taint, for even her narration is free of the violence that the vampire represents. She is thus the prize for which the men battle Dracula and a symbol of the Good for which everyone has fought. Not precisely a symbol of motherhood and apple pie—the novel is, after all, a nineteenth-century English novel—she does nonetheless symbolize progress, legal and scientific thought, and Christian tolerance—indeed the entirety of Western European thought in Stoker's time.

The narration of Mina's friend, Lucy Westenra, helps shed light on Mina's narration and also reveals why Lucy is Dracula's victim. Lucy is introduced by a series of letters that she exchanges with Mina and later by the journal that she keeps in imitation of Mina. Unlike Mina, who has had to work for a living and who has adopted the progressive philosophy associated with the world of work, Lucy seems to be an anachronism. Her letters are filled with accounts of her daily activities, of visits "to picture-galleries and for walks and rides in the park" (73) and of her relationship with three young men who seek her hand in marriage. That she sees herself as weak is evident in her reason for choosing to marry Arthur Holmwood: "I suppose that we women are such cowards that we think a man will save us from fears, and we marry him" (77). Thus she appears to be perfectly conventional, although a brief confession to Mina reveals that dissatisfaction lurks beneath her conventional exterior: "Why can't they let a girl marry three men, or as many as want her, and save all this trouble? But this is heresy, and I must not say it" (78).

Indeed, Lucy's narration reveals that she herself isn't aware of her desire to rebel against her upbringing. Mina, aware of the vampire's embrace, is horrified but also confesses to her attraction: "I was bewildered, and, strangely enough, I did not want to hinder him. I suppose it is a part of the horrible curse that such is, when his touch is

29

on his victim" (342–43). Lucy's account never reaches this level of awareness, indeed, any level of awareness of what had happened to her. After sleepwalking to the cemetery in Whitby where Dracula first touches her, she remembers nothing. Although "full of vague fear" (143), knowledge of Dracula's presence in her life never reaches her consciousness. She thus represents total innocence—perhaps ignorance—and dies because neither she nor the people around her are aware of what threatens her until it is too late. Because of her death, Lucy's narration ends at the novel's midpoint.

Dr. John Seward, the young head of a London madhouse, is the last of the main narrators that Stoker introduces. In addition to a diary that he keeps on a phonograph—a technological device with which Stoker was familiar, notes Stoker's biographer Barbara Belford—Seward reveals himself mainly through letters and telegrams to both his old friend Holmwood and his mentor Dr. Van Helsing. Like most of the characters who battle Dracula, Seward seems to be an advocate of modern technology in its many guises. More important, however, Seward is initially the spokesman both for science and for the value of scientific thinking.

Stoker's use of nineteenth-century science is examined in more detail in chapter 8, but here I focus on how science affects narration. Parts of Seward's diary reveal his feelings for Lucy, but the bulk of his narration is an extremely detailed account of one patient, R. M. Renfield, whom he identifies as "zoöphagous" (life-eating). Seward admits that his interest in Renfield originally stems from the scientific desire to discover knowledge: "Had I even the secret of one such mind—did I hold the key to the fancy of even one lunatic—I might advance my own branch of science to a pitch compared with which Burdon-Sanderson's physiology or Ferrier's brain-knowledge would be as nothing" (95). Thus, Seward reveals that he is consciously modeling himself on fellow scientists, and his journal reveals the good scientist's attention to accurate detail.

Other characteristics of Seward's narrative include belief in things that he can see and, like Jonathan Harker, the frequent disbelief of his sanity. For example, Van Helsing argues that the vampire's greatest power is that people in the rational nineteenth century no longer believe in supernatural forces, that "in this enlightened age, when men believe not even what they see, the doubting of wise men would be his greatest strength" (380). Seward, the single scientific narrator in the group, constantly questions his sanity when his experiences go against his scientific knowledge even after he observes Lucy in the cemetery and encounters Dracula on several occasions: "I sometimes think we must be all mad and that we shall wake to sanity in strait-waistcoats" (327). Despite occasionally questioning his sanity, however, Seward comes to trust in the evidence that they accumulate. For example, he and Van Helsing share their suspicions that Mina Harker is coming under Dracula's control, although they agree not to mention their suspicions to the others until the time is right.

Case, one of the few critics to examine Stoker's narrative strategy in detail, looks specifically at the intersection of science with narration, arguing that both science and narrative involve organizing "experience or data into a meaningful form, which can then be deployed to practical ends." She notes that Van Helsing's reluctance to share "hypotheses or information, even with Seward, until they have fully 'ripened' into authoritative coherence ... also underlines the linkage of scientific and narrative authority," for both science and narrative are "founded on the benevolently manipulative withholding of information and/or the self-conscious staging of its revelation at the moment when it will carry greatest force."[8] The practical end for the two scientists is the destruction of the vampire, and they usually refuse to offer up their hypotheses until they have significant proof. For example, Van Helsing goes to elaborate lengths to prove to Holmwood, Seward, Morris, and the incredulous reader that Lucy has become a vampire. At the conclusion, they do not need to prove that Mina is free from Dracula's taint, for Dracula's destruction is accompanied by visual evidence of her return to purity, as Morris notes in his dying breath: "Now God be thanked that all has not been in vain! See! the snow is not more stainless than her forehead! The curse has passed away!" (444). Presumably, this proof should be sufficient for the reader as well, although Harker's final note encourages readers to question this evidence:

I took the papers from the safe where they had been ever since our return so long ago. We were struck with the fact, that in all the mass of material of which the record is composed, there is hardly one authentic document; nothing but a mass of type-writing, except the later note-books of Mina and Seward and myself, and Van Helsing's memorandum. (444)

A similar question about the truthfulness of the record is raised by material that precedes chapter 1:

How these papers have been placed in sequence will be made manifest in the reading of them. All needless matters have been eliminated, so that a history almost at variance with the possibilities of later-day belief may stand forth as simple fact. There is throughout no statement of past things wherein memory may err, for all the records chosen are exactly contemporary, given from the standpoints and within the range of knowledge of those who made them. (xxiv)

Thus, if Harker's concluding note raises the issue of truth and proof, this note (presumably written by Harker as well because he seems to be the keeper of the papers) raises the issue of subjectivity and the fact that the recorded events will be difficult to believe.

The events may indeed be difficult to believe, but Stoker's narration is designed to prove that the impossible is possible and, thus, to draw readers away from their ordinary, rational, scientific, and legal world and into a world in which the impossible is believable. For that reason, Stoker brings his narrators together at the novel's midpoint. Van Helsing shows Holmwood, Seward, and Morris that Lucy has become a vampire while Harker's journal documents Dracula's careful plans to come to England.

The combination of narrative voices, that is, the narrative strands that are ultimately linked physically in the typewritten manuscript of Jonathan and Mina Harker, is important also because it represents the collective wisdom of the late nineteenth century—male and female, Catholic and Protestant, science and law. That even Renfield's apparently insane ravings are ultimately brought into the narrative is additional proof of the existence of vampires. As Van Helsing notes so poignantly (right before he and the rest of the men mistakenly deny Mina the protection of that combination), the power of combination is denied to the vampire:

> We have on our side power of combination—a power denied to the vampire kind; we have sources of science; we are free to act and think; and the hours of the day and the night are ours equally. In fact, so far as our powers extend, they are unfettered, and we are free to use them. (288)

The combined information, knowledge, strength, and financial resources that enable the narrators to overcome Dracula is reinforced by a narrative strategy that emphasizes the need for unity and teamwork. Only when the reader has access to all the information strands does the story of Dracula and his opponents make any sense.

The story of the battle against Dracula is the story of a group's victory, so it is appropriate that Dracula himself remains silent throughout, his language recorded only by those who have sworn to destroy him. Dracula himself leaves almost no written record of his plans to come to England except a few brief notes to Harker, and there is little material evidence of his existence in England except the boxes of earth, documents, keys, and "a clothes brush, a brush and comb, and a jug and basin—the latter containing dirty water which was reddened as if with blood" (357). Van Helsing and his followers destroy Dracula's belongings so that, at the end of the story, there is literally nothing left of him: "It was like a miracle ... and almost in the drawing of a breath, the whole body crumbled into dust and passed from our sight" (443). Silenced by the narrative structure, Dracula is literally disposed of at the conclusion of the novel. It is a truism to acknowledge that history is written by the victors, but *Dracula* is the history of those who conquer the vampire, a history that celebrates the collective power of present law, science, scholarship, religion, technology, and capital against the lonely primitive who is finally tracked back to his lair and destroyed.

Because this discussion of narration in *Dracula* concludes with the important recognition that Dracula is himself silenced by the text, it is important to note the one other character who is ultimately silenced by the text. That character is Mina Harker, one-time collator and narrator of the tale as we see it. In one of the best discussions of narration in the novel, Case notes that Mina takes over when her husband relapses after seeing the count in London and temporarily abdicates his responsibility for the story:

> Mina decides that it is time to gain a better command of her husband's story by reading the sealed journal.... Jonathan has become the helpless, disordered center around which interpretive efforts must be mobilized by others.[9]

Case sees this move on Mina's part as a move to acquire power, an interpretation with which I agree, and observes in addition that Mina assumes "the role of master-narrator which Van Helsing, concerned ... with the withholding of unripe knowledge, has thus far declined."[10] Case concludes by observing that Mina's power as a narrator represents a challenge to all the men in the novel and that this challenge "leads to her subsequent silencing and incapacitation."[11]

Case's brilliant analysis adds a sinister interpretation to the conclusion of *Dracula*, a conclusion that silences both Dracula and Mina. Thus, a skillful reader might understand that both Dracula and Mina are silenced by the collective strength of the band that had combined forces against them. Rescued from a vampirish existence, Mina Harker is nonetheless silenced by her husband and her friends. In fact, she is not even given the last word of her own story, for her husband adds a final postscript that attests to its fantastic nature: "We could hardly ask any one, even did we wish to, to accept these as proofs of so wild a story" (444–45).

5

Traveling to Transylvania:
Race, Space, and the British Empire

Dracula begins as a travel diary, with the youthful Jonathan Harker's account of his journey from Germany to Transylvania. It quickly becomes a social and political commentary that enables readers to evaluate Stoker's thoughts on a number of subjects, including racial issues, the problems relating to Home Rule in Ireland, and British imperialism in general. All these subjects would have been on the minds of people in England during 1897, the year of Victoria's Diamond Jubilee. Perhaps in no other year would the average resident of England have been so aware of the problems of the empire on which the sun never set, problems delineated by Stephen D. Arata:

> The decay of British global influence, the loss of overseas markets
> ... the economic and political rise of Germany and the United
> States, the increasing unrest in British colonies and possessions,
> the growing domestic uneasiness over the morality of imperial-
> ism—all combined to erode Victorian confidence in the in-
> evitability of British progress and hegemony.[1]

Furthermore, as Cannon Schmitt notes,[2] Stoker would have been aware that imperial pursuits meant that Europe was poised on the brink of war at the time he was writing *Dracula*:

> Written at the zenith of European imperial expansion, between the Berlin Conference of 1884 and the outbreak of the Boer War in 1899, *Dracula* takes shape ... when widespread armed conflict ... over territorial possessions, although temporarily suspended, must have appeared inevitable.[3]

Arata and Schmitt thus agree with Richard Wasson, who writes in "The Politics of *Dracula*," one of the first scholarly examinations of the novel, that readers "cannot help but be stirred by the political implications of *Dracula*."[4] These and similar studies reveal both the importance of reading *Dracula* as much more than a fantasy in which heroic individuals battle evil vampires and the importance of seeking out the social and cultural problems that underlie the gothic fantasy.

Harker's diary seems to begin innocently enough, as he describes his experiences with ethnic foods and observes the picturesque dress and behavior of the peasants. The diary quickly reveals Harker's underlying prejudice against practically everything that he regards as foreign, however. What initially appears exotic quickly becomes suspect and ultimately evil, as Harker changes from tourist to patriot. Crossing the Danube, he has an impression of "leaving the West and entering the East" (1), and he later observes that he had read that "every known superstition in the world is gathered into the horseshoe of the Carpathians" (4). The language suggests his innate distrust of everything foreign, a distrust that eventually erupts in violence as he stands over Dracula's prostrate body and imagines the Other as monstrous:

> This was the being I was helping to transfer to London, where, perhaps, for centuries to come he might ... satiate his lust for blood, and create a new and ever-widening circle of semi-demons to batten on the helpless. The very thought drove me mad. A terrible desire came upon me to rid the world of such a monster. (67)

That Harker fears the foreigner as a bloodsucker bent on invading England is significant in a novel that is filled with numerous references to historical invasions and to the rise and fall of nations. Dracula, for example, tells Harker of the numerous invasions of his homeland, "ground fought over for centuries by the Wallachian, the Saxon, and the Turk" and explains that the soil had been "enriched by the blood of men, patriots or invaders" (30). Informing his English pupils of the feats of the historical Dracula, Van Helsing describes heroic endeavors against the Turks who had invaded Dracula's homeland. Although most of the invasions in the novel take place in Eastern Europe, Stoker reminds readers that England had been invaded when he has Mina, while a tourist in Whitby, mention that the abbey there had been "sacked by the Danes" (84). These references to violent foreign invasions are significant during a period in which England was intent on preserving her colonial holdings and may even suggest the fear of reverse colonization.

These fears of the outsider are reinforced later in the novel when Van Helsing compares their battle against Dracula to a holy war in which they must destroy their opponent: "But to fail here, is not mere life or death. It is that we become as him; that we henceforward become foul things of the night ... preying on the bodies and the souls of those we love best" (287). Thus, *Dracula* resembles a battle of opposing cultures in which the Western European characters associate the vampire with dirt, lack of humanity, darkness, the absence of morality, and predation and pledge themselves to destroy all that threatens their beliefs.

Looking at Stoker's original plan for the novel suggests that he originally intended to focus more specifically on cultural differences. Belford, who notes a number of significant changes between Stoker's working notes and the published book, indicates that he originally planned to have Harker stop off in Munich,[5] a decision that would have diluted the extreme contrast between Transylvania and England. Not only does the change eliminate roughly 100 pages of material, but it also enabled Stoker to focus on extreme differences between West and East, civilized England and primitive Transylvania, rationalism and superstition, progress and stagnation. These extremes would have been less dramatic if Stoker had begun in Germany, another country in Western Europe. Furthermore, Arata adds that Transylvania would have resonated with racial and political overtones in 1897 because Transylvania was associated with the " 'Eastern Question' that so obsessed British foreign policy in the 1880s and '90s" and because the entire region was known for "political turbulence and racial strife."[6] As *Dracula* now stands, the novel opens with Harker's being confronted immediately with the awareness of centuries of political turmoil.

Historically, much of the turmoil in Eastern Europe had been exacerbated by cultural and racial differences. Dracula speaks with pride of his distinct racial heritage when he informs Harker that his veins are filled with "the blood of many brave races who fought as the lion fights, for lordship" (39). Although it is almost impossible to trace Dracula's lineage through the "whirlpool of European races" that he mentions, it is important to underline that his racial background includes a number of non-European strains, including that of Attila, the one ancestor that Dracula names and of whom he is most proud. Thus, Stoker identifies Dracula at the outset as racially Other.

A number of recent studies point out that focusing on the vampire, an entirely different type of being, is one way for Stoker to examine racial issues. Looking at race in *Dracula* leads Judith Halberstam, in "Technologies of Monstrosity: Bram Stoker's *Dracula*,"[7] to conclude that Stoker was influenced by nineteenth-century anti-Semitic discourse that "makes the Jew a monster with bad blood" and to add that "the vampire as represented by Bram Stoker bears some relation to the anti-Semite's Jew."[8] To support her argument, Halberstam focuses on Dracula's distinctive appearance and foreign sexuality and concludes that he "is a composite of otherness that manifests itself as the horror essential to dark, foreign, and perverse bodies."[9]

Other scholars have noted a racial fear closer to home and one with which Stoker as an Anglo-Irishman would have been familiar. Arata reminds readers that the English regarded the Irish as primitive, dirty, and violent and that Britain's treatment of the Irish was often more brutal than their treatment of colonial peoples.[10] Robert Tracy sees the vampire as a symbol of Stoker's fears of the native Irish and argues that he shared that fear with Joseph Sheridan Le Fanu, creator of *Carmilla*, another vampire tale by an Anglo-Irish writer and one with which Stoker was clearly familiar.[11] According to Tracy, both Le Fanu and Stoker were members of the Protestant Anglo-Irish ruling class who found in vampire legends "metaphors for their class's anxieties about the unhyphenated Irish, who were emerging from centuries of suppression to demand political and economic power." Tracy adds that the Anglo-Irish "feared intermarriage with the Irish, which would lead to racial degeneration."[12]

Another scholar who examines the impact of Stoker's Irishness on *Dracula* is Schmitt, who argues that the combination of "racialism and nationalism promotes ... the proliferation of grisly stories: tales of murder, cannibalism, bloodsucking."[13] Schmitt reminds readers of Stoker's loyalty to England and uses as evidence Stoker's first book, *The Duties of Clerks of Petty Sessions in Ireland*, a treatise on duty that he wrote while he was employed as a civil servant in Dublin Castle. Looking at the similarities in these two works might cause readers to conclude that Jonathan Harker, full of loyalty to both his employer and his country, resembles the young Irish civil servant who wrote this treatise whereas Dracula and his vampire brides are like the native Irish, degenerate and needing to be controlled.

Seeing Dracula and vampires in general as racial threats that require control or containment initially makes a great deal of sense, for the characters in *Dracula* focus on the ways that vampires differ from their human opponents. Furthermore, the characters' emphasis on racial difference is consistent with late nineteenth-century imperialist ideology as Elaine Showalter summarizes it in *Sexual Anarchy: Gender and Culture at the Fin de Siècle*:

> Racial boundaries were among the most important lines of demarcation for English society; fears not only of colonial rebellion but also of racial mingling, crossbreeding, and intermarriage, fueled scientific and political interest in establishing clear lines of demarcation.... After General Gordon's defeat by an Islamic fundamentalist, the Mahdi, at Khartoum in 1885, many saw signs that the Empire was being undermined by racial degeneration and the rebellion of the "lower" races. Late Victorian science, especially ... physical anthropology, devoted itself to establishing the legitimacy of racial differentiation and hierarchy.[14]

Joseph Bristow's discussion of Africa in *Empire Boys: Adventures in a Man's World*[15] also examines the fact that racist ideology depends on emphasizing the differences in peoples:

> The image of the African ... had been increasingly distorted.... As the nineteenth century wore on, evangelists, explorers, and anthropologists ... put together a picture of Africa as the most savage place in the world.... ethnologists were measuring African heads to establish a hierarchy of racial types. In France, anthropometry and ... craniometry began with Paul Broca's investigations of 1861. Francis Galton's hereditarian interests in measuring skulls and bodies were put on public display in the laboratory he established at the International Exposition of 1884.[16]

There are no Africans in *Dracula* although Stoker does kill off African characters in at least two novels, *The Mystery of the Sea* and *The Lair of the White Worm*. He also kills off two non-English characters in *Dracula*, Quincey Morris (an American) and Dracula. That racist beliefs were such a distinct part of the ideology of imperialism is clear in the analyses of both Showalter and Bristow. It is also clear that racism and the accompanying fear of other racial groups were intensified by hostile relations between England and her colonies at the turn of the century.

One very specific fear that is associated with racism is atavism, or the psychological and social regression of a colonial ruler to the level of the colonized primitive people supposedly under his control, a fear that is often addressed in fin de siècle adventure literature. For example, Patrick Brantlinger argues that atavism "is one of the three central themes of imperial Gothic"[17] and uses Kurtz's regression in *Heart of Darkness* as one of his primary examples. Brantlinger also mentions that documented cases of backsliding were well known and uses as evidence the dozen possible models that Ian Watt lists for Kurtz in *Conrad in the Nineteenth Century*.[18] Brantlinger does not mention atavism in conjunction with *Dracula* and instead associates Stoker with one of the other themes of imperial Gothic, "the theme of invasion, often in the form of demonic powers from the past as in ... Stoker's tales of terror."[19] Although the present chapter touches on the fear of invasion in *Dracula*, I believe that the threat of atavism is also evident in Van Helsing's warning about the possibility of becoming like Dracula, "foul things of the night like him—without heart or conscience, preying on the bodies and the souls of those we love best" (287). Certainly, a number of characters in *Dracula* do regress. Upon becoming a vampire, Lucy begins to resemble the vampire-women when she starts to prey on children, and even the determined Mina Harker is identified by the three vampire-women as their sister. Indeed the entire novel suggests that the lines of demarcation between supposedly fixed categories are extremely tenuous. This tentativeness on Stoker's part suggests that he was also uncertain about standard nineteenth-century racist ideology, a system of beliefs that suggested distinct lines of demarcation.

Among the scholars who suggest that Stoker's views on race are complex are both Arata and Glover. Arata points out numerous similarities between Dracula and the English characters, whereas Glover reminds readers that Stoker was friends with Gladstone and that Stoker and Gladstone were committed both to Home Rule for Ireland and to a Liberal political philosophy in general:

> Stoker lived through some of the formative years of Irish nationalism and, though he died nearly a decade before independent statehood was achieved, he was a cautious but convinced advocate of Irish Home Rule from at least his early twenties.[20]

Thus Stoker was inclined to believe that the Irish were capable of governing themselves, a belief that indicates that he saw the Irish as similar to their English rulers. Furthermore, Belford observes that Stoker's experience as Inspector of Petty Sessions acquainted him with the fact that the Irish farmers suffered under the English landlord system and argues that Stoker "set about to reform and unify the system, gathering together diverse data into ... *The Duties of Clerks of Petty Sessions in Ireland.*"[21] Not only did Stoker advocate self-governance for Ireland, but he was also an early advocate of a united nations and delivered a well-publicized speech on the subject when, as auditor of the Historical Society at Trinity College, he opened the annual meeting of that group on 13 November 1872.

Finally, even the study of exotic peoples ultimately brings nineteenth-century thinkers back home, as Bristow notes:

> For Victorians, the picture of ... Africa brought together a number of interrelated European anxieties about religion, sexuality, and history.... Their untiring journeys ... were ... travels into two troublesome zones ... the urban squalor of major cities, and ... the unknown underworld passages occupying the labyrinthine depths of the supremacist psyche.[22]

People who expect differences when examining racial issues in the nineteenth century are often confronted with similarities. A similar pattern occurs in *Dracula*, because the novel begins by noting differences in peoples as well as differences between human beings and vampires but ultimately encourages readers to confront the similarities among peoples and the similarities between people and vampires.

Early in the novel, Harker had wondered whether Dracula were human—"What manner of man is this, or what manner of creature is it in the semblance of man?" (48)—and he generally identifies Dracula as a monster. However, when Harker notices with shock that Dracula is wearing the suit of clothes that Harker had worn as he traveled to Transylvania, he wonders whether the local people will see Dracula dressed in his clothing and blame him for any "wickedness" that Dracula might commit. Indeed, events reveal that the local people cannot tell the difference between the two, because the agonized mother who comes to the castle seeking her child looks up at Harker and cries out, "Monster, give me my child!" (61). Although Harker is at quite a distance, the brief scene nonetheless emphasizes that the woman sees similarities in Harker and Dracula, not differences.

Moreover, although Harker sees Dracula as an exotic foreigner, it is clear that Dracula, once in England, doesn't generally appear foreign. Dracula had purchased English books and newspapers to avoid looking like "a stranger in a strange land" (28), and he generally manages to avoid seeming strange. Thomas Bilder, keeper in the Zoological Gardens, had obviously conversed with Dracula, but Bilder mentions nothing about Dracula's exotic dress or accent, and the various teamsters whom Harker interviews comment only on Dracula's great strength, not on the fact that he is foreign or racially different. Indeed, I can think of only two occasions when anyone notices anything foreign about Dracula: On first meeting him, Jonathan Harker notices that he speaks "excellent English, but with a strange intonation" (23). Later, when he hurries to leave England, Dracula wears a straw hat, which "suit not him or the time" (376), a fashion gaffe that even the sailors notice.

Finally, the most significant revelation of the similarity between Harker and Dracula is that they share attitudes as well as clothing. The historical Dracula had repulsed the Turkish invaders from his homeland, and Jonathan Harker is equally eager to repel the invading vampire from his. Furthermore, although both Dracula and Harker are proud of their military prowess, the novel reveals that both are equally adept at guerrilla warfare and subterfuge. Accusing Dracula of being a warlord and monster who preys on the bodies and souls of the innocent, Harker is nonetheless pictured on several occasions standing over the body of the prostrate vampire, a significant example of role reversal. At one point, Harker looks down at the unconscious vampire and comments on Dracula's monstrous Otherness, then strikes at him with the edge of a shovel that the workers had left. It seems clear that Harker notices only differences between himself and Dracula, but the reader should notice a marked similarity.

Stoker intended for readers to note the resemblances in Dracula and Harker, which may explain the brief scene in which Harker glances in the shaving mirror and fails to see Dracula standing behind him until Dracula taps him on the shoulder: "This time there could be no error, for the man was close to me, and I could see him over my shoulder. But there was no reflection of him in the mirror! The whole room behind me was displayed; but there was no sign of a man in it, except myself" (34). The standard interpretation of this scene is that the absence of a reflection reveals Dracula to be a supernatural being or indicates that creatures without souls have no mirror reflections. Instead, Stoker may have been showing that Harker and the other Western European characters see only one aspect of Dracula and thus never really see him at all. As a result, the mirror yields only Harker's version of what is there just as the narration presents only one version of the truth, an issue that is covered in the previous chapter. Readers, on the other hand, are capable of grasping a larger perspective.

Readers will also note marked similarities between vampires and humans after the baptisms of Lucy and Mina. Unbeknownst to the other members of the group, Van Helsing and Seward confer about the physical changes they note in Mina. Later, as he and Mina approach Dracula's castle, Van Helsing comments on changes in Mina's appearance and behavior. Uncertain about the extent of the change, he wonders whether he can trust her.

All these scenes reveal that the real distinctions between vampires and humans are negligible. Nothing, however, connects the two more directly than Stoker's repeated emphasis on blood. Although the multiple blood transfusions that Van Helsing performs on Lucy would most likely have killed her because physicians in Stoker's day knew nothing of blood types, Stoker uses these blood transfusions to connect his characters. By the time of her death, Lucy has the blood of four men flowing through her veins, an act that serves as her marriage to them. Underlying the fact that sharing blood unites two people is Dracula, who explains to Mina Harker that she is now his bride: "And you, their best beloved one, are now to me, flesh of my flesh; blood of my blood; kin of my kin; my bountiful wine-press for a while; and shall be later on my companion and my helper" (343).

Moreover, Dracula and the other vampires are not the only bloodsuckers in the novel. Not only is Mina caught in the act of drinking blood, with her lips smeared with Dracula's blood, but Van Helsing reveres Dr. Seward for having once sucked contaminated blood from his wound. The characters are thus all linked together both by blood and by habit.

Numerous readers have commented on the significance of blood in *Dracula*, but no one is more insightful than Anne McWhir about the way that blood links all the characters together.[23] In "Pollution and Redemption in *Dracula*," McWhir begins her analysis with Renfield's quotation of the Old Testament that "the blood is the life" and observes that the blood in *Dracula* connects "different categories to each other, making distinctions difficult between the pure and the impure, between rituals of social consolidation and their demonic counterparts."[24]

Finally, all the characters in the novel are linked by the birth of little Quincey Harker. Not only does the child combine the blood of all the characters through his mother and father, but he also shares Dracula's blood, which his mother had drunk. Moreover, because Dracula, in drinking Lucy's blood, had also drunk the blood of the other men in the novel, young Quincey Harker also has the blood of Van Helsing, Arthur Holmwood, Quincey Morris, and Dr. Seward coursing through his veins. No wonder that Harker can comment on his son as a unifying presence: "His bundle of names links all our little band of men together; but we call him Quincey" (444).

Once again, as we attempt to come to terms with *Dracula*, we discover that the novel is rarely as simple as it initially appears. It is tempting to label *Dracula* a racist text because so many of the characters make statements that seem so blatantly racist by late twentieth-century standards. Labeling the novel as racist does not do it justice, however, even though evidence both from the novel and from Stoker's own life suggests that he was influenced by racist ideology. The Western European characters justify their violent treatment of Dracula and the vampire-women on the grounds that vampires are different, are nonhuman, and Stoker extended that violent treatment to other racial groups in several other novels, including *The Mystery of the Sea* and *The Lair of the White Worm*. Halberstam notes furthermore that Stoker was friends with the explorer and translator Richard Burton, who wrote a treatise that revived the "blood libel against Jews in Damascus."[25] Stoker's *Personal Reminiscences of Henry Irving* includes a horrible anecdote in which Burton justifies killing a young Arab:

> I remember ... hearing of how at a London dinner-party he told of his journey to Mecca.... he had to pass as a Muhammadan; the slightest breach of the multitudinous observances of that creed would call attention, and suspicion at such a time and place would be instant death.... He saw that a lad had noticed him and was quietly stealing away. He faced the situation at once, and coming after the lad ... suddenly stuck his knife into his heart.... I asked him once about ... the killing. He said it was quite true, and that it had never troubled him.... "The desert has its own

laws, and there—supremely of all the East—to kill is a small offence. In any case what could I do? It had to be his life or mine!"…. Then he went on to say that such explorations as he had undertaken were not to be entered lightly if one had qualms as to taking life. That the explorer in savage places holds, day and night, his life in his hand; and if he is not prepared for every emergency, he should not attempt such adventures.[26]

Stoker's anecdote about Burton is not precisely racist, but it does suggest that, for Burton, the life of the Other has little value.

Although it is undoubtedly true that some of Stoker's ideas about race were connected directly to the racist ideology that was common at the turn of the century, it is equally true that *Dracula* moves far beyond the mere sense of racial differences and hostility to recognize similarities. Thus, whereas Harker does not see Dracula's face in the mirror and therefore does not recognize how much he himself resembles the monster that he despises, *Dracula* does encourage readers to see ourselves in the novel, to recognize our connectedness with the Other, whether that Other is Dracula, Mina, or little Quincey Harker, who in fact connects everyone.

Looking at *Dracula* along these lines helps explain why Stoker's fiction can include such disparate ideas. On the one hand, he supports Home Rule in Ireland and argues against extreme nationalism. On the other, his fiction often makes disparaging remarks about nonwhite characters. These seemingly inconsistent beliefs were nonetheless common for people like Stoker who were grounded in traditional views but who nonetheless looked to a future that would be unlike the present. A fin de siècle writer, Bram Stoker often combined extremely conservative views with progressive ideas, a trait that makes him difficult both to classify and to understand.

6

Those Monstrous Women:
A Discussion of Gender in *Dracula*

Since the rebirth of interest in *Dracula* in 1972, a number of excellent articles have examined Stoker's treatment of his women characters. This issue is especially important to our understanding of the novel because the condition of women changed radically during Stoker's lifetime, and *Dracula* addresses these changes very directly. Stoker grew up during a period that insisted on Separate Spheres for men and women, arguing that men were more temperamentally suited for work outside the home while women were, therefore, suited to domestic work. In the decades prior to Stoker's work on *Dracula*, however, the roles of men and women had changed as more and more women entered the professions and the educational establishments, a pattern that escalated during the 1890s. Stoker's fiction reveals that he was clearly mulling over these changes, as were most of his contemporaries. Their deliberations produce interesting discussions by gender-conscious writers at the end of the twentieth century as well.

These twentieth-century essays on the women in *Dracula*, mostly by feminist critics, have been joined, since the mid-eighties, by other studies that examine the larger treatment of gender issues in the novel. Although many of these later studies analyze vampires as symbols for late-nineteenth-century apprehensions about homosexuality, others point out other complex anxieties about gender in the novel.

Any discussion of gender in *Dracula* should begin with the startling realization that, of the vampires in the novel, five are female while only one, Dracula, is male. Because the novel's "villains," or vampires, are disproportionately female while the novel's heroes are disproportionately male, the attention of many readers quickly turns to questions of gender. Although Jonathan Harker's diary occasionally touches on gender issues (such as his references to the immodest dress of women peasants and his plans to collect recipes for his fiancée) and suggests that he is comfortable with the notion of Separate Spheres for men and women, a more dramatic introduction to gender issues is the scene, early in the novel, in which he is surrounded by three vampire women who are determined to suck his blood. The scene contrasts vividly with Harker's brief references to women, most of which indicate that men and women behave very differently.

Realizing that he is Dracula's prisoner, Harker decides to explore the castle and finds himself in the women's section, "where, of old, ladies had sat and sung and lived sweet lives whilst their gentle breasts were sad for their menfolk away in the midst of remorseless wars" (50). The description is full of gendered language that reinforces Harker's sense that men and women are very different: women are "sweet," "gentle," and "sad" whereas men fight in "remorseless wars." Moreover, the description suggests that women remain passively at home while their menfolk are off somewhere.

What happens next horrifies Harker, for he is accosted by "three young women, ladies by their dress and manner" who surround him and prepare to kiss him:

> There was something about them that made me uneasy, some longing and at the same time some deadly fear. I felt in my heart a wicked, burning desire that they would kiss me with those red lips. (51)

Harker, who has been thinking of Mina, obviously feels guilty about his desire, but the scene reveals that he is worried about more than his momentary unfaithfulness:

Those Monstrous Women: A Discussion of Gender in Dracula

> There was a deliberate voluptuousness which was both thrilling and repulsive, and as she arched her neck she actually licked her lips like an animal, till I could see in the moonlight the moisture shining on the scarlet lips and on the red tongue as it lapped the white sharp teeth.... I closed my eyes in a languorous ecstasy and waited—waited with beating heart. (52)

The scene emphasizes three characteristics that are not ordinarily associated with women in the nineteenth century—sexuality, aggression, and bestial behavior. Harker is saved only by the return of Dracula, who brings with him a substitute for Harker, a bag from which emerges "a gasp and a low wail, as of a half-smothered child" (53). Belford, who is prone to interpret Stoker's entire life according to material in *Dracula*, describes this scene as one that reveals a great deal about Stoker[1] and notes that it depicts "the worst nightmare—and the dearest fantasy—of Victorian men: union with a pure girl transformed into a sexually aggressive woman."[2] Belford's emphasis on sexuality is undoubtedly correct, for the brief scene resonates with sexually charged language. The scene also points readers to thinking about some basic inconsistencies in the way nineteenth-century thinkers regarded sexuality.

Although nineteenth-century thinkers tended to regard women as less sexually oriented than men, the presence of large numbers of prostitutes in urban areas meant that people were aware that at least some women were sexual beings. Certainly, in the decades preceding Stoker's work on *Dracula*, debates over the Contagious Diseases Acts kept the subject of prostitution before the eyes of people in England, and the association of prostitutes with disease implied a concern with contagion. In *Walking the Victorian Streets: Women, Representation, and the City*, Deborah Epstein Nord[3] uses language that suggests that the fear of being infected by contact with a prostitute is remarkably similar to the fear of being infected by contact with a vampire:

> This widely used imagery of contamination and pestilence culminated in ... the appropriately named Contagious Diseases Acts, passed by Parliament in the 1860s in an effort to contain the spread of venereal disease ... by forcing prostitutes to undergo

49

medical inspection. The acts themselves gave weight to the powerful notion that such women existed to ensnare men and to defile their bodies with disease.[4]

Nord's study of women in urban areas makes no reference to vampires, but *Dracula* is full of references that imply that vampirism resembles a contagious disease. Moreover, many of the characters in *Dracula* suggest the connection between vampirism and sexuality. For example, Harker's sense that a sexually attractive woman is dangerous is reinforced by all the men in the novel. Here is Van Helsing at the conclusion of the novel during which he confronts the first of the three vampire-women:

> She lay in her Vampire sleep, so full of life and voluptuous beauty that I shudder as though I have come to do murder. Ah, I doubt not that in old time ... many a man who set forth to do such a task as mine, found at the last his heart fail him, and then his nerve.... Then the beautiful eyes of the fair woman open and look love, and the voluptuous mouth present to a kiss—and man is weak. And there remain one more victim in the Vampire fold; one more to swell the grim and grisly ranks of the Un-Dead! (436)

The passage resonates with Van Helsing's fear of contagion, a fear made even more horrifying by the fact that the vampire-woman also appears to be desirable.

Harker is troubled not only by the vampire-women's sensuality, however, but also by their lack of maternal feelings and by their treatment of the baby that Dracula brings as a Harker-substitute.

The three vampire-women appear in a mere half dozen pages and are important primarily to introduce values and beliefs that *Dracula* will explore more fully in Lucy Westenra and Mina Harker, English women who are also infected by the vampire taint.

Before setting Dracula's enigmatic brides aside, however, it is necessary to consider the significance of the fair woman who is given such prominence in the early scene. Because the two dark women resemble Dracula, they are generally interpreted as relatives, sisters perhaps, and therefore appear even more horrifying because they suggest incest, a particularly perverse form of sexuality. The fair woman does not resemble Dracula, though, and Harker notes of her, "I seemed somehow to know her face, and to know it in connection with some dreamy fear" (51). Critics have speculated that this fair woman is especially frightening to Harker because she resembles Lucy Westenra, Harker's mother, or simply a typical English girl. Having studied Stoker's notes, however, Belford provides a much simpler answer, observing that Harker recognizes her because she is the Countess Dolingen, whom he met in the chapter that was subsequently deleted. Belford adds that the "inconsistency was never caught in the editing process. An original line explains everything: 'As she spoke I was looking at the fair woman and it suddenly dawned on me that she was the woman—or her image—that I had seen in the tomb on Walpurgis Night.' "5 I wish that other questions regarding Stoker's treatment of women were as easily answered, including the question of whether the fair vampire is responsible for Dracula's vampirism or vice versa.

There is no doubt that Stoker links Lucy Westenra with the three brides, for once Lucy becomes a full-fledged vampire, she is equally voluptuous and lacking in maternal sentiments. Seward, who had only four months earlier proposed marriage to Lucy, looks at her with horror after her transformation:

> The sweetness was turned to adamantine, heartless cruelty, and the purity to voluptuous wantonness.... With a careless motion, she flung to the ground ... the child that up to now she had clutched strenuously to her breast, growling over it.... There was a cold-bloodedness in the act which wrung a groan from Arthur; when she advanced to him with outstretched arms and a wanton smile, he fell back and hid his face in his hands. (257)

Lucy was not always a monster, as the above excerpt from Seward's diary suggests, and even the name that Stoker gives her suggests her dual nature. Wicke is one of the many critics to point to one part of that duality: "If one considers her name, Luce, light and illumination, emanating out of the West-enra, she is clearly an overdetermined being, more than a woman, a civilizational cause."6 She thus symbolizes a particularly Western type of goodness. In addition to signifying goodness, however, the name Lucy also suggests another fallen angel, Lucifer. More important in terms of this discussion of gender issues, the ease with which Lucy changes from innocent maiden to voluptuous vampire reveals a great deal about Victorian ideas on female behavior. The rapidity of the changes implies a degree of latent evil that is easily unleashed by sexual initiation.

Unlike her old friend, Mina Harker, who has had to work for a living, Lucy has led a pampered existence, and her letters are full of references to picture-galleries, to walks and rides in the park, and to slang. It seems a trivial portrait of a superficial young woman except that Stoker hints that there is more to her character. For example, she admits to being a "horrid flirt" (78) and to flaunting her three marriage proposals: "Just fancy! THREE proposals in one day! Isn't it awful!" (74). Even more suggestive are Stoker's hints at something more rebellious in Lucy's nature. For example, she accepts Arthur's proposal before consulting her mother and confesses, prior to accepting his proposal, a desire to marry all three men who have proposed to her: "Why can't they let a girl marry three men, or as many as want her, and save all this trouble? But this is heresy, and I must not say it" (78).

In Lucy, Stoker paints a portrait of a young woman who is all convention on the surface, certainly of one who seems to accept the traditional roles of wife and mother that are laid out for her. During the day, Lucy never admits her rebellion about the constraints placed on women, but at night her rebellion surfaces as she wanders around Whitby in her sleep and eventually meets Dracula. Kline comments on the significance of Lucy's sleepwalking and notes that Lucy's father, who had died from a heart ailment, had suffered from somnambulism his entire life. She explains that sleepwalking was regarded as "an inherited (degenerative) form of neurosis" at the time and adds that the Westenra "family's heart disease suggests at the same time, symbolically, that the 'heart,' or spiritual center, of the family was corrupt."[7] Kline adds that meeting Dracula brings out Lucy's own latent corruption, for "she gradually begins to acquire the sharp canine incisors of the wild, bloodthirsty beast she is in the process of becoming."[8]

Because Lucy never realizes her own desire to escape from rigid nineteenth-century constraints on women, she cannot protect herself

Those Monstrous Women: A Discussion of Gender in Dracula

from temptation when it occurs. She is thus two times a victim, first of Dracula's seduction, and second, of her society's desire to purify her. Her death, which concludes the second part of the novel, is bloody and horrifying, more so because it is brought about by her fiancé and by three other men who had loved her:

> The Thing in the coffin writhed; and a hideous, blood-curdling screech came from the opened red lips.... But Arthur never faltered.... his untrembling arm rose and fell, driving deeper and deeper the mercy-bearing stake, whilst the blood from the pierced heart welled and spurted up around it. His face was set, and high duty seemed to shine through it.... There, in the coffin lay no longer the foul Thing that we had so dreaded and grown to hate that the work of her destruction was yielded as a privilege to the one best entitled to it, but Lucy as we had seen her in her life, with her face of unequalled sweetness and purity. (262–64)

That this scene takes place on 29 September, one day after the day on which Lucy and Arthur were to have been married, reinforces the fact that the scene reestablishes normal gender patterns along with Lucy's "sweetness and purity." If the novel had ended with this scene, it would be tempting to conclude that Stoker was an antifeminist who simply hated women or that he was a traditionalist who hated the sexually assertive women who were gaining prominence in the 1890s.

Stoker's portrait of Mina Harker, however, adds several additional dimensions to his treatment of women in the novel. Although Mina appears to be a traditional woman because she defers to her husband's judgment (even when she thinks his judgment is mistaken) and looks forward to motherhood, she is also experienced in nontraditional fields and becomes one of the leaders in the quest against Dracula.

Instead of preying on children, Mina looks forward to motherhood and, before the novel concludes, manages to "mother" all the men. Attempting to explain this emphasis on motherhood, Kline connects Judeo-Christian mythology with turn-of-the-century sociology and notes that Hebrew theology made woman the cause of all sin and argued that the pain of childbirth is women's payment for Eve's sin.

Kline adds that "Christians ... were more optimistic and hopeful: woman's suffering in giving birth would also be the source of her salvation.... Mina, too, is ultimately redeemed by her childbearing."[9] Kline's theory is interesting except that Mina is redeemed by Dracula's death, not by the birth of her son. Furthermore, Mina and Jonathan are married on 24 August. Bearing a child in November, only three months later, would throw Mina's unimpeachable virtue into question. Therefore, I have always assumed that Harker's note, which says that "our boy's birthday is the same day as that on which Quincey Morris died" is either an oversight on Stoker's part or a reference to the anniversary of the date on which both Dracula and Quincey Morris died.

Moreover, Kline's assertion that Mina is a kind of Eve figure doesn't take into account the fact that Stoker attempts, in the character of Mina Harker, to combine both traditional and modern views of womanhood. Most assuredly, Mina is a motherly figure, but she is far more than that.

One characteristic that sets Mina apart from her more traditional friend, Lucy, is the fact that Mina has had to work for a living even though it is in a field (teaching) that had been acceptable for impoverished gentlewomen for much of the nineteenth century. That she appears to resent her job, which she describes as "trying" (71), and seems eager to improve her condition by learning new skills, such as typing and shorthand, connects her to more modern women, those who wish to see all the professions opened to women. She admits, however, that she has learned a great deal about appropriate behavior for women by teaching in a school for girls:

> Jonathan was holding me by the arm, the way he used to in the old days before I went to school. I felt it very improper, for you can't go on for some years teaching etiquette and decorum to other girls without the pedantry of it biting into yourself a bit. (214)

Attention to decorum explains why Mina is ashamed that Lucy has gone out without shoes, but it also reveals more about the differences in the two women. The conscious Lucy is also compliant, adhering to conventional behavior for young women and obediently wearing Van Helsing's garlic flowers for their medicinal value. Mina's appropriation of proper behavior is more than mere attention to surface behavior, however, as is evident in the scene in which she is discovered with Dracula.

Unlike Lucy, who remembers only the bittersweet sensation of yielding to Dracula, Mina is horrified by the encounter: "I was bewildered, and, strangely enough, I did not want to hinder him" (342). Even though Mina had previously done everything possible to assist in the battle against Dracula and had collated all the documents belonging to members of the group, she now intensifies her efforts, offering to let Van Helsing hypnotize her so that the group can follow Dracula's movements and even asking them to kill her if she becomes too great a threat to their safety. Even at the conclusion, when it is apparent that Dracula is gaining power over her life, she refuses to join the three women-vampires:

> They smiled ever at poor dear Madam Mina; and as their laugh came through the silence of the night, they twined their arms and pointed to her, and said in those so sweet tingling tones.... "Come, sister. Come to us. Come! Come!" In fear I turned to my poor Madam Mina, and my heart with gladness leapt like flame; for oh! the terror in her sweet eyes, the repulsion, the horror, told a story to my heart that was all of hope. God be thanked she was not, yet, of them. (434)

What distinguishes Mina from the other women in the novel are her level of intellectual awareness and her own horror at sexual aggression.

As the previous scene makes clear, Mina never shares the aggressive sexuality of the other vampire-women. She does, however, share much of their rebellion against social constraints. The three women in Dracula's castle obviously chafe against his masculine authority and rebel against him whenever they have the opportunity. Similarly, Lucy Westenra longs to marry three men and slips out of her house to enjoy the forbidden pleasures of the night. The biggest difference between Mina and the other women is that Mina is aware of her rebellion. For example, when Van Helsing and the other men choose to protect her rather than let her in on their plans, she notes that such chivalrous protection of women is misguided:

> All the men, even Jonathan, seemed relieved; but it did not seem to me good that they should brave danger and, perhaps, lessen their safety—strength being the best safety—through care of me; but their minds were made up, and, though it was a bitter pill for me to swallow, I could say nothing, save to accept their chivalrous care of me. (293)

Later events prove that Mina's judgment is correct, for Dracula would not have found her such ready prey if she had been in the company of the other vampire hunters and if Dr. Seward hadn't given her an opiate to help her sleep, another decision that Mina rightly questions:

> He very kindly made me up a sleeping draught, which he gave to me, telling me that it would do me no harm, as it was very mild.... I have taken it, and am waiting for sleep, which still keeps aloof. I hope I have not done wrong, for as sleep begins to flirt with me, a new fear comes: that I may have been foolish in thus depriving myself of the power of waking. I might want it. (312, Stoker's ellipsis)

Mina's judgment is accurate in other events as well: she is in many ways the unrecognized leader of the group even though the men do not always want to accept her wisdom. Not only does she put their papers in order so they can track Dracula's past movements, but she determines the most likely route for his return to his castle, and she manages to hold the group together even as she comes increasingly under Dracula's control. Glover, in examining Mina's behavior, observes that she takes on a role that Stoker's contemporaries would have seen as masculine:

> Though *Dracula* enacts a struggle for the possession of women's bodies and ruthlessly punishes the least hint of precocious female sexuality ... it is a novel which temporarily recruits a woman into a man's place, arming Mina "like the rest" with "a large-bore revolver" as our heroes move in for the final kill.[10]

Those Monstrous Women: A Discussion of Gender in Dracula

Alternatively, one might argue that Stoker allows Mina to adopt a very human role, beyond the rigid gender conventions of the late nineteenth century, and that only at the conclusion, when the predator has been safely laid to rest, does she return to a traditional woman's role. In fact, one might even argue that the very rigid nineteenth-century roles for men and women put women at risk, for the physicians never inform Lucy of what is threatening her, and the chivalrous treatment of Mina isolates her and makes her easy prey.

Stoker's treatment of Mina allows me to question the wisdom of the many social constraints placed on traditional women. Furthermore, Mina's character also combines aspects of the traditional woman's role with characteristics associated with more modern women who, during the nineteenth century, sought equality with men. Although women who criticized the traditional roles that were permitted to them agreed on little else except their criticism of tradition, they were often lumped together at the end of the nineteenth century as New Women.

Karl Beckson, in *London in the 1890s: A Cultural History*, indicates that the women who saw themselves as New Women were rebelling against traditions:

> In art and in life, the New Woman insisted on alternatives to the traditional roles for women. Her smoking in public, riding bicycles without escorts, or wearing "rational dress" ... was not the result of mere whim or self-indulgence but of principle, for she was determined to oppose restrictions and injustices in the political, educational, economic, and sexual realms in order to achieve equality with men.[11]

Dracula reveals that Mina is clearly aware of the New Woman, just as any reasonably educated woman in the 1890s would have been. Instead of sharing the interests of those women, however, Mina seems to regard their rebellion as silly and misguided, as the following excerpt from her diary reveals:

> Some of the "New Women" writers will some day start an idea that men and women should be allowed to see each other asleep

before proposing or accepting. But I suppose the New Woman won't condescend in future to accept; she will do the proposing herself. And a nice job she will make of it, too! (120)

Mina's sarcasm about the forward behavior of the New Women is certainly consistent with the views held by those who adhered to the traditional roles for men and women. Whereas Angelica Hamilton-Wells, a New Woman in Sarah Grand's 1893 bestseller *The Heavenly Twins*, had successfully proposed to her husband, Stephen Norman, the heroine of Stoker's *The Man*, (1905) proposes marriage to a totally unsuitable man and nearly ruins her life and the life of the man who truly loves her. Glover argues that this "disastrous offer of marriage ... both partially repeats and substantially critiques the same act"[12] in *The Heavenly Twins*, an argument with which I concur. In fact, I suspect that Stoker might have been thinking of *The Heavenly Twins*, of Hardy's *Jude the Obscure*, or of Grant Allen's even more notorious *The Woman Who Did* when he has Mina criticize the New Woman.

Mina's criticism and her later acceptance of marriage and motherhood might imply that she is an entirely traditional woman. Readers should remember her resentment when the men attempt to protect her and also the fact that Stoker has their plan go radically wrong once Mina is out of the picture. Mina is thus "new" so far as intellectual ability goes, traditional so far as sexual behavior is concerned. Therefore, it seems to me that Stoker is more concerned with the aggressive sexuality of the vampire-women than with their gender, an interpretation that is consistent with Stoker's close friendships with women, including Ellen Terry, Geneviève Ward, Pamela Colman Smith, Mary Elizabeth Braddon, and George Egerton (the pen name of the New Woman writer Mary Chavelita Bright). Many of these women were considered advanced for their time.

Before leaving this discussion of the women in *Dracula*, it is appropriate to see that Dracula himself is often linked to female sexuality. Usually perceived by his opponents as a warlord and aristocratic male seducer, he is also, as Anne Williams demonstrates, associated with female energy and wields his masculine power on "behalf of the 'female'—darkness, madness, blood":

Those Monstrous Women: A Discussion of Gender in Dracula

> Dracula is the "other" of the horror plot, the monster that must be destroyed.... In contrast to Van Helsing and his band of enlightened scientific rationalists, Dracula is a creature of the dark, of madness, and of ancient superstition. Most surprisingly ... he is also associated with that most powerful and persistent "Other," the female.
>
> In an ... undeniable pattern of allusions, Stoker himself links the monster with ... female power and perversity. Dracula arrives ... on a ship called the "Demeter" and departs on ... the "Czarina Catherine."[13]

Furthermore, Dracula is almost always associated with women. In Transylvania, he lives with three women whom he loves, as he retorts when challenged by the saucy blonde vampire: "Yes, I too can love; you yourselves can tell it from the past" (53). He later taunts his English opponents by referring to his intimate relationships with their women: "Your girls that you all love are mine already" (365). Finally, in a very peculiar scene, he is presented as a nursing mother when he forces Mina to drink blood from his breast:

> With that he pulled open his shirt, and with his long sharp nails opened a vein in his breast. When the blood began to spurt out, he took my hands in one of his, holding them tight, and with the other seized my neck and pressed my mouth to the wound, so that I must either suffocate or swallow some of the—Oh my God! my God! what have I done? (344)

This peculiar mixing of gender identities and sexual relationships enables readers to see that Stoker associated Dracula with the sexuality of women, a social issue of which he and his contemporaries were increasingly aware. Moreover, seeing Dracula as "Other" in sexual ways enables readers to understand what Maurice Richardson meant when he described *Dracula* in "The Psychoanalysis of Ghost Stories,"[14] one of the first twentieth-century examinations of the novel, as a "kind of incestuous, necrophilious, oral-anal-sadistic all-in-wrestling match."[15]

I can not abandon this discussion of gender and sexuality in *Dracula* without mentioning the recent studies that have interpreted Stoker's master-vampire as a homosexual. Among them is Nina Auerbach, who describes the novel as "a compendium of fin-de-siècle phobias."[16] Auerbach is nonetheless quick to point to Dracula's obvious homosexuality: "The British 1890s were haunted not only by the Undead, but by a monster of its own clinical making, the homosexual."[17]

Along with a number of other critics, Auerbach connects Dracula with Stoker's old friend Oscar Wilde, whose trial was going on while Stoker was working on *Dracula*. In fact, Auerbach argues that "Dracula's primary progenitor is not Lord Ruthven, Varney, or Carmilla, but Oscar Wilde in the dock."[18]

In " 'A Wilde Desire Took Me': The Homoerotic History of *Dracula*," Talia Schaffer points to numerous parallels between *Dracula* and the Wilde trial. Schaffer overstates her case (she argues, for example, that Stoker started writing *Dracula* "one month after his friend, rival, and compatriot Oscar Wilde was convicted of the crime of sodomy"[19] although Stoker's collected notes show that he had started working on the novel five years earlier), but her argument contains a certain persuasiveness. She notes, for example, that Dracula is not to be confused with the historical individual but "represents the ghoulishly inflated vision of Wilde produced by Wilde's prosecutors; the corrupting, evil, secretive, manipulative, magnetic devourer of innocent boys."[20] She adds one more bit of evidence involving the novel's narration: "The novel's composition, with its newspaper clippings and emphasis on journalistic techniques like shorthand, obliquely acknowledges its debt to the Wilde-saturated newspapers of April, May, and June, 1895."[21]

Finally, Schaffer notes that the secrecy associated with nineteenth-century homosexual life, including nocturnal lives and the absence of servants "become ominous emblems of Count Dracula's evil."[22] At this point, I feel compelled to add that such secrecy would have been involved in any kind of nonmarital sex, including the types of perverse sex noted by Richardson. In fact, part of what has made *Dracula* such a popular text is its ability to speak to a number of different kinds of people over the past hundred years. Thus the vampires in *Dracula* continue to frighten (and titillate) generations of readers because vampires represent the monstrous other. To an English culture at the end of the nineteenth century that celebrated masculinity, heterosexuality, Western culture, and rationality, these vampires were feminine, homosexual, Oriental, and instinctual. Indeed Elaine Showalter shows how this otherness is linked to sexuality in her introduction to *Sexual Anarchy: Gender and Culture at the Fin De Siècle*:

> The 1880s and 1890s, in the words of the novelist George Gissing, were decades of "sexual anarchy," when all the laws that governed sexual identity and behavior seemed to be breaking down.... During this period both the words "feminism" and "homosexuality" first came into use, as New Women and male aesthetes redefined the meanings of femininity and masculinity.... The fin de siècle was also a period of sexual scandals. In England, they ranged from the trial and acquittal of the notorious brothel-keeper Jeffries in 1884, and the sensational journalistic series on child prostitution of W. T. Stead, "The Maiden Tribute of Modern Babylon," in 1885, to the exposé of the Cleveland Street male brothel in 1889. All of these scandals changed the level of public awareness about sexuality and engendered a fierce response in social purity campaigns, a renewed sense of public moral concern, and demands, often successful, for restrictive legislation and censorship.[23]

During a period so concerned with the connection between sexuality and crime, it would have been easy to associate almost any kind of sexuality with the monstrous Other, the vampire.

Looking back at Stoker's treatment of both women and vampires almost tempts me to conclude that Stoker was a traditionalist about gender issues, that he longed for the time when the roles of men and women were distinct and when attempts to deviate from those prescribed roles met with repression, hostility, and death. On the other hand, Stoker clearly celebrated Mina Harker, a woman who both chafes against those rigid roles and manages to accomplish heroic acts when she is outside that traditional role. Thus, Stoker created a work that is somehow larger than the values and beliefs of its characters, a work that manages to criticize many of the traditional beliefs that its characters hold dear. As a result, readers remember both Dracula and Mina as powerful figures, not simply as characters who are either destroyed or returned to their proper niche when the novel ends.

Jonathan Harker quotes Van Helsing at the conclusion and reminds readers of the complexity of Mina's character:

> This boy will some day know what a brave and gallant woman his mother is. Already he knows her sweetness and loving care; later on he will understand how some men so loved her, that they did dare much for her sake. (445)

With these words that reinforce traits in Mina that are perceived as masculine at the end of the nineteenth century ("brave" and "gallant") as well as her more traditional feminine characteristics ("sweetness" and "loving care"), Stoker concluded the novel. That *Dracula* continues to speak to readers poised on the threshold of a new century about values that are important to us in fact reinforces Stoker's modernity as well as his depiction of traditional views.

7

This Way Madness Lies:
Nightmares, Schizophrenia, Religion,
and Confusion about Boundaries

Looking at insanity in *Dracula* leads us to focus on Renfield. Although the madman is a relatively minor character, his desire to absorb as many lives as possible initially connects him to Dracula while his sacrifice to protect Mina eventually links him to the other Western European characters. Furthermore, although Renfield is the character in the novel who is most obviously insane, readers should also recognize that the question of sanity is pervasive in the novel. Dr. Van Helsing sorrows over an insane wife; entire sections of *Dracula* take place in Dr. Seward's London mental asylum; and many of the characters in the novel at one time or other question their sanity or at least the truth of what they see. Even more important, perhaps, the fact that various characters question their sanity encourages readers to examine larger questions of truth and falsehood in the novel, questions that touch on the novel's treatment of nineteenth-century religion, science, and even aesthetics.

When readers first meet R. M. Renfield, he is apparently a new patient of Dr. Seward's, for Seward seems to be just beginning his case history. When Mina asks to see him, Renfield provides additional background material, telling her that he had been incarcerated by his friends for believing that he can indefinitely prolong life by consuming a multitude of live things. He admits that his belief makes him dangerous to others, and the reader sees him in action in the scene in which he breaks into Seward's office, cuts the doctor's wrist with a dinner knife, and licks the blood from the floor. Renfield's desire for blood also links him to Dracula whom he initially calls master and admits to the asylum, where the count attacks Mina. Ultimately, however, Renfield betrays Dracula when he discovers that the vampire has been drinking Mina's blood, and he is killed for this betrayal.

Although Renfield's behavior at the beginning of the novel would meet anyone's definition of insanity, he is apparently shocked into sanity when he realizes what it means to drink the blood of another living being. This realization causes him to ally himself with the other Western European characters. Other characteristics also link him to the group that battles Dracula. Evidently an educated man, the 59-year-old Renfield is aware of Van Helsing's scientific work and had been a member of the same club as the senior Lord Godalming. Furthermore, like most of the other Western European characters, he keeps a "notebook in which he is always jotting down something. Whole pages of it are filled with masses of figures, generally single numbers added up in batches, and then the totals added in batches again, as though he were 'focusing' some account" (92). In Renfield's case, the jottings seem to apply to his "experiments" with catching and eating live creatures, experiments that connect him most directly to Dr. Seward, the specialist in diseases of the brain and the most clearly scientific person in *Dracula*.

That the distinction between sanity and insanity is not always clear becomes evident in Renfield's development. Seward describes Renfield's consumption of flies, spiders, and even sparrows, but Renfield is shocked back to what most readers would call sanity when he realizes that Dracula had drunk Mina's blood and is therefore destroying her soul as well. Arguing that he is "a sane man fighting for his soul" (298), Renfield begs Dr. Seward to release him from the asylum. Dr. Seward, who remembers the Renfield of a few days before and who frequently comments on the bizarre changes in Renfield's behavior, understandably refuses to grant his request.

At the time of his death, Renfield seems to be sane. An earlier scene suggests the difficulty of distinguishing sanity and insanity, however, and reminds readers that Stoker suggests overlap in other categories that seem to be mutually exclusive, including the sacred and the profane. In the scene in which an apparently sane Renfield begs for his freedom, Dr. Seward, who has observed Renfield talking to Mina, notes that Renfield "addressed himself to the question with the impartiality of the completest sanity" (283). Renfield goes on to explain that the Scriptural phrase, "For the blood is the life," has been adapted by the vendor of a certain nostrum who has "vulgarised the truism to the very point of contempt" (283). Wolf's note on this line indicates that this nostrum is "surely 'Hughes's Blood Pills,'" which, in an advertising brochure ... claimed that 'The Blood being therefore the Life of the living Body, it stands to reason that if it is poisoned, you poison the whole system, and eventually destroy the life of the man.' "[1] Whether Wolf is correct about the exact reference is irrelevant, because the entire passage points the reader to connections between categories that are ordinarily treated as quite distinct. That Scripture is used to advertise a patent medicine muddles the distinction between the sacred and the secular, though, just as events in the novel cause readers to question the distinction between sanity and insanity, legal and illegal activities.

Renfield is, of course, the most extreme case in *Dracula*, but various other characters also remind readers that such rigid distinctions are arbitrary as those characters worry about encroaching madness and their fragile hold on sanity. Pondering Lucy's condition, Seward queries, "What does it all mean? I am beginning to wonder if my long habit of life amongst the insane is beginning to tell upon my own brain" (174). Confronted with the unbelievable events surrounding Lucy's death, he compares himself to one of his patients: "At present I am going in my mind from point to point as a madman, and not a sane one, follows an idea" (237). Finally, while thinking about the plan to track Dracula home, Seward again questions his sanity and the sanity of his companions: "I sometimes think we must be all mad and that we shall wake to sanity in strait-waistcoats" (327).

Whereas Seward's knowledge of insanity comes from his profes-sional experience, other characters have more visceral awareness of the fine line that distinguishes sanity from insanity. Most pronounced in this group is the solidly business-like Harker, whose experiences in Transylvania bring him perilously close to madness. Even before he meets Dracula, Harker begins to question the truth of what he is see-ing, generally phrasing the question in terms of sleep and conscious-ness instead of sanity and insanity: "I think I must have fallen asleep and kept dreaming of the incident, for it seemed to be repeated end-lessly, and now looking back, it is like a sort of awful nightmare" (18). Arriving at Dracula's castle, he confesses, "I must have been asleep, for certainly if I had been fully awake I must have noticed the approach to such a remarkable place" (21). Later he wonders whether he had imagined the encounter with the three vampire-women: "I must have fallen asleep; I hope so, but I fear, for all that followed was startlingly real—so real that now, sitting here in the broad, full sunlight of the morning, I cannot ... believe that it was all sleep" (51). Harker even-tually comes to accept that he must believe that which is unbelievable and escape from Dracula's castle. After his escape, the reader hears nothing of Harker until Mina receives a letter from Sister Agatha that reveals that Harker is "suffering from a violent brain fever" and that "in his delirium his ravings have been dreadful" (131). Like Renfield, he is at least temporarily insane.

At least one of Stoker's biographers wonders whether this inter-est in insanity may have come from a situation close to Stoker, because his brother Thornley's wife, Emily Stoker, was sequestered in a distant wing of their Dublin residence because of mental illness. Observing that Stoker focuses on insanity throughout *Dracula*, Belford argues that Van Helsing's reference to a mad wife echoes Thornley's situa-tion.[2] Stoker's explorations of insanity in *Dracula*, especially the diffi-culty in determining who is sane and who is not, go far beyond any-thing merely autobiographical, however. In fact, *Dracula* often leads readers to recognize that conventional distinctions among categories are not so simple at all. For example, when Van Helsing tells the oth-ers that Lucy had bitten the children, Seward, who had earlier questioned his own sanity, responds, "Madness were easy to bear compared with truth like this" (239).

Seward's observation about truth and insanity brings readers to one of the crucial questions asked in *Dracula*, indeed in any work of literature: What is truth? Is truth associated with the science in which so many of the characters place their trust? with the law? with religious faith? Although the question of truth is examined in somewhat different ways in both the chapter on narration and the chapter on science, this chapter examines sanity, religion, and aesthetics, all topics that fall outside the ordinary boundaries of proof. In other words, these topics all rely on the belief in things that lie beyond proof rather than in ideas that can be proven by scientific experiment.

There is no doubt that the Western European characters are at least nominal Christians or that the English characters are adherents to the Church of England. Jonathan Harker, for example, is uncomfortable when the innkeeper's wife gives him a rosary: "I did not know what to do, for as an English Churchman, I have been taught to regard such things as ... idolatrous, and yet it seemed so ungracious to refuse an old lady" (9). More devout than her husband, Mina often thanks God for her good fortune. This devotion and her belief that she had "tried to walk in meekness and righteousness" makes Dracula's attack on her all the more horrifying. Initially filled with revulsion at the attack, she ultimately gains consolation in the thought that the attack is simply a way of testing their faith. In fact, she reveals to her husband "that it is in trouble and trial that our faith is tested—that we must keep on trusting; and that God will aid us up to the end" (345).

Moreover, characters often allude to Scripture. That they sometimes misinterpret the Scriptural passages or misremember them may mean nothing more significant than that they are all secular people with a limited understanding of the text on which their faith is based. Inexact recollection and imprecise interpretation does, however, reinforce that the distinctions between religious faith and magic are as muddled as the distinctions between sanity and insanity.

One important Scriptural reference is Renfield's refrain, "For the blood is the life" (283). Not only does Renfield here echo numerous

Old Testament prohibitions against drinking the blood with the flesh (Genesis 9:3–6; Leviticus 17:10–11; Deuteronomy 12:23), but he reveals that he doesn't understand the Scriptures, which specifically forbid the drinking of blood. Thus Renfield echoes the precise Scripture that condemns both himself and the literal vampires in *Dracula*.

References to marriage are pervasive in *Dracula*, and several of them also allude to Scripture. Renfield, explaining his lack of interest in flies and spiders to Dr. Seward, replies enigmatically, "The bridemaidens rejoice the eyes that wait the coming of the bride; but when the bride draweth nigh, then the maidens shine not to the eyes that are filled" (133–34). Anticipating that Dracula is coming to him, Renfield seems to echo John the Baptist and John's promise that someone greater will follow:

> You yourselves bear me witness, that I said, I am not the Christ, but I have been sent before him. He who has the bride is the bridegroom; the friend of the bridegroom, who stands and hears him, rejoices greatly at the bridegroom's voice; therefore this joy of mine is now full.[3]

Finally, even Dracula alludes to Scripture when he confesses to Jonathan Harker that he doesn't want to be "a stranger in a strange land" (28), a reference to Moses's son, born of the Midian woman, Zipporah, who was named Gershom to indicate that he was born when his father was a stranger in a strange land.

In addition to these allusions that suggest that his characters are at least somewhat familiar with Scripture, Stoker indicates that his Western European characters are influenced by the ritual and sacraments of the Christian church, including marriage, burial, and Holy Communion. These sacraments are often perverted, however. For example, the blood transfusions that Van Helsing performs on Lucy become a substitute for marriage. After Arthur mentions that the transfusion of his blood has made Lucy his wife, Van Helsing breaks down in hysterics and later observes to Seward that Lucy, who had received the blood of four men, is therefore a "polyandrist." That the exchange of blood is a substitute for marriage as well as a perversion of Holy Communion is perhaps even more clear in the case of Mina Harker, for Dracula reminds her that their exchange of blood has made them one flesh: "And you ... are now to me, flesh of my flesh; blood of my blood; kin of my kin ... and shall be later on my companion and my helper" (345). The language echoes several biblical references to marriage (Genesis 2:24; Mark 10:8; and Ephesians 5:25–33) as well as the marriage rituals of various denominations. It is also significant that the blood exchange echoes the words of Jesus at the Last Supper (Matthew 26:26–29; Mark 12:22–25; Luke 22:19–20), words that point Christians to the communion of Christ and his believers. In *Dracula*, however, the blood exchange represents a most unholy alliance.

Recognizing that she has been polluted by her relationship to Dracula, a relationship both bigamous and heretical, the devout Mina asks her companions to read the Order for the Burial of the Dead over her before they leave England. This service combines with the fact that the Host scars her forehead to indicate that Mina is now officially dead and, therefore, beyond the power of conventional religion. Only Dracula's death will bring her back within the fold. It is, however, a most heretical scene, for it suggests that Mina's faith is inadequate and that the power of Dracula somehow outweighs the ability of God to grant grace to those who believe in Him.

In addition, the Western European characters often rely on religious symbols, although frequently in ways that are different from those for which the symbols were intended. For example, Van Helsing places a small gold crucifix on Lucy's corpse, and he provides all his followers with crucifixes to use as weapons against Dracula. Van Helsing also uses the Host in a variety of ways, some of which are arguably blasphemous: He molds the Host into a putty to seal off Lucy's tomb and also crumbles it to sterilize Dracula's boxes of earth. Because the Host represents the body of Christ and is intended as a symbolic reminder of Jesus's sacrifice, using it in these ways is closer to magic than to religion. That Van Helsing also tells his followers that he has an indulgence from the Church to use the Host in such ways runs counter to Roman Catholic practice, for the indulgence is used only to protect people from temporal punishment for sins that they have already committed and for which they have already been forgiven. Under no circumstance would Van Helsing receive an indulgence for a sin he is going to commit.

Dracula also echoes pagan beliefs that have been absorbed by the Judeo-Christian tradition. Van Helsing explains to his followers that vampires must be buried in sacred earth: "For it is not the least of its terrors that this evil thing is rooted deep in all good; in soil barren of holy memories it cannot rest" (292). The deaths of both Renfield and Quincey Morris are akin to the ancient practice of the blood sacrifice. Renfield explains that he confronts Dracula to protect Mina: "I had heard that madmen have unnatural strength; and as I knew I was a madman—at times anyhow—I resolved to use my power.... I held tight; and I thought I was going to win, for I didn't mean Him to take any more of her life" (335). Because the attendant hears Renfield call out to God, the reader may also assume that Renfield, in the moments before his death, has consciously shifted his allegiance from Dracula to God and has offered himself as a sacrifice. Morris's sacrifice is even more deliberate: "I am only too happy to have been of any service.... It was worth for this to die.... Now God be thanked that all has not been in vain! See! the snow is not more stainless than her forehead! The curse has passed away!" (444). Like Renfield, Quincey admits that he has not always lived a good life, so his sacrifice presumably redeems himself as well as Mina.

Finally, *Dracula* includes faint echoes of very primitive fertility religions. Williams comments that Jonathan Harker arrives in Transylvania on 5 May, St. George's Eve, and notes that because this day was "an ancient fertility festival sacred to the Great Mother," St. George's Eve was a time "when the female principle is (unconsciously) felt to be in ascendance."[4] Lucy's staking occurs on Michaelmas (29 September), a day dedicated to St. Michael, one of the chief angels in the Christian tradition, and also a day associated with the harvest. Finally, Dracula is destroyed on 6 November, a day devoted to St. Leonard, another dragon slayer. Found in myths throughout the world, dragon slayers usually signify that the forces of light or good have overcome evil or darkness.

In *Dracula*, references to dragons and dragon slayers are significant for historical reasons too. The historical Vlad of Wallachia acquired the name Dracula because the Holy Roman Emperor had designated his father the leader of the Order of the Dragon, a semimilitary, semimonastic order established to fight the Turks. Because the Wallachian word for dragon (and, by an interesting historical twist, for devil as well) is *dracul*, the historical Vlad Dracula was literally "the son of the dragon." That the word *dracul* would have connected him to the devil as well is an interesting etymological fact.

What is significant to me about these religious references, some overt and some veiled, is that they all point to the fact that it is often as difficult to distinguish genuine religion from magic or superstition as it is to distinguish madness from lucidity or, in the case of the historical Vlad, patriotism from sadism. Nonetheless, Van Helsing asks his followers to believe in things for which there is no proof, telling them that he "heard once of an American who so defined faith: 'that faculty which enables us to believe things which we know to be untrue'" (237).

Furthermore, Van Helsing's emphasis on faith occurs at a time of waning religious faith, although Joel N. Feimer argues correctly, in "Bram Stoker's *Dracula*: The Challenge of the Occult to Science, Reason, and Psychiatry,"[5] that this increased secularization had begun much earlier:

> Once Descartes observed that the only thing of which he could be certain was the fact that he was thinking... the existence of all entities that could not be verified, quantified, or otherwise measured by scientific instruments was cast into doubt. Among these discredited essences were God, the Devil and his legions, and a corresponding host of occult activities and principles. By degrees, as the centuries progressed, it became foolish and then certifiably pathological to believe in such things as gods, demons, witches, and vampires.[6]

To connect this strand of my interpretation to the earlier part of this chapter, religious faith therefore becomes equivalent to insanity in the minds of many rationalists, even more insane in the nineteenth century when the Darwinian theory of evolution by natural selection seems to direct people away from God and toward material explanations. Chapter 8 addresses the presence of nineteenth-century science in *Dracula* more directly, however.

What concerns me here are the interesting connections between sanity, religion, and gothic fiction. In fact, *Dracula* blurs the conventional distinctions between realistic fiction and the gothic novel in that it features obviously supernatural characters and events within a form that might be described as almost documentary realism.

Much of the commentary on *Dracula* focuses on its connections to particular genres, especially to the gothic and to various kinds of fantasy. For example, Garret Stewart, in " 'Count Me In': *Dracula*, Hypnotic Participation, and the Late-Victorian Gothic of Reading,"[7] observes that Stoker wrote *Dracula* during "the broadspread reflowering of the gothic in the fin de siècle" and notes "proliferating antirealisms of the period—including fantasy, science fiction, the exotic adventure tale, certain exemplars of the New Woman fiction, and the prose of decadence in its various forms."[8] Glover also notes "that the genres that Stoker prefers and in which he excels—Gothic horror, romance, utopias" are those that depart from "the idioms of classical realism" and consequently "lend themselves to the ruses of fantasy."[9] Kline indicates that Stoker's yet unpublished working papers for *Dracula* indicate that he originally intended to write a vampire story but apparently changed his mind when he was about a third of the way through. Kline then observes that the novel moves away from fantasy to realism when the story of Jonathan Harker's captivity ends and the scene shifts to England. At this point Stoker introduced a new group of characters and changed the aesthetic direction of the novel:

> [T]he nightmarish atmosphere is supplanted by a comparatively sober ... mood; time and place assume sudden significance and the narrative structure changes. The story is no longer told through the personal diary of a young man ... who most of the time is uncertain of whether the events he is describing actually occurred ... but through the documents ... of characters who assure one another of their sanity.... Having made this change in his narrative method, Stoker allows Jonathan's diary to appear in retrospect as ... evidence in the criminal case his new cast of protagonists begins to prepare against the "Un-Dead."[10]

Although I am tempted to agree with Kline in that *Dracula* does seem to move away from the borderline insanity of Harker's journal to the consensus or sanity of the later sections, I do not see the aesthetic shift that Kline notes. In fact, what I see in *Dracula* is that it consistently encourages readers to question conventional distinctions. Is it sane or insane to believe in vampires or in miracles? Looking at one such conventional distinction, Cyndy Hendershot, in "Vampire and Replicant," offers a profound reminder that human beings often confuse consensus with truth:

> Thus what is accepted as reality—or as realism in art—is in fact an acceptance of the dominant ideology of a given society as ontological truth. Realism as an aesthetic stance may be read as an endorsement of hegemony rather than an attempt to scrutinize its "reality." This is a juncture at which the Gothic and sf meet in their refusal to reproduce ideological "reality," and their attempts either to imagine alternative realities or to contaminate the ideologies already in place.[11]

Like many other works of fantasy, *Dracula* blurs conventional boundaries. Are Jonathan Harker and R. M. Renfield sane or insane? Are Van Helsing and his followers devout practitioners of religion or believers in magical rites? Is *Dracula* more influenced by the nineteenth-century realistic novel or by the gothic? Does science or does religion provide readers with the best way to live their lives? By blurring a number of conventional distinctions, *Dracula* thus encourages readers to look more deeply at their world, a world in which the demise of genuine religious faith was sometimes masked by a growing interest in supernatural fiction.

8

For the Blood Is the Life:
Dracula and Victorian Science

Whereas the previous chapter addresses the religious connotations of blood and of blood drinking, this chapter begins by looking at the way that Stoker uses blood to comment on Victorian developments in science, including the blood transfusions that figure so prominently in *Dracula*. From there, the chapter moves to larger questions about the significance of science in the novel, including the presence of numerous scientists and pseudoscientists, and the rise of science as a powerful discipline during Stoker's lifetime, one that had already begun to influence political and social thought.

Stoker's interest in both science and in blood came initially from personal experience. An invalid for the first seven years of his life, Stoker was treated during this period by his uncle William, who was affiliated with Dublin's Fever Hospital and House of Recovery and who, according to Belford would have bled the child, either by opening the temporal artery or by applying leeches.[1] Knowing this biographical information makes it tempting to look at the scenes in which various characters lie powerless at the hands of a vampire in terms of the child's helplessness in the hands of his powerful uncle. This biographical reading is not necessarily wrong, but it doesn't begin to explain the richness and complexity of *Dracula*.

Stoker's connection with the scientific community remained throughout his adult life. Three of his four brothers (Thornley, Richard, and George) also chose medicine as a career, and both Farson and Belford comment on Stoker's close friendships with Thornley and George. Moreover, Glover indicates that Stoker's working notes for *Dracula* show that he consulted Thornley before writing about Renfield's fatal injuries; Glover adds that Stoker also consulted Thornley about other medical and scientific material in the novel.[2]

Unlike his uncle and brothers, Stoker was apparently more interested in theoretical science, for he graduated from Trinity College, Dublin, in 1871 with a degree in science and stayed on for a master's degree in pure mathematics. That it took him three years to complete the advanced degree may mean, however, that he lost his enthusiasm for pure mathematics. Whatever the reason for his career move away from science and mathematics, Stoker's novels suggest that he continued to be interested in both and to educate himself in a variety of fields. For example, Stoker went on to study law and passed the bar in 1890. His namesake in *Dracula*, Dr. Abraham Van Helsing, is a veritable Renaissance man with advanced degrees in a wide variety of fields, including law, philosophy, and literature in addition to medicine.

Dracula reveals Stoker's continued interest in science. Coursing through its pages and linking its various parts is blood, a subject that fascinated nineteenth-century scientists and physicians alike. Kline observes that Darwin thought that genetic material circulated in the bloodstream and argues that, for Darwin, therefore, "the blood was indeed the life" because it contained the information that communicated the animal's or human's mental and physical makeup. Kline adds that Darwin's nephew, Francis Galton, began blood transfusions in 1870 to test Darwin's theory but that Galton eventually rejected the theory when his "publicly condemned series of vivisections, in which he transferred blood from one species of animal to another in order to influence the offspring, miserably failed."[3] Despite Galton's failure, though, Kline indicates that blood fascinated scientific thinkers and experimenters until heredity was finally explained in the twentieth century. Stoker didn't seem especially interested in the hereditary aspects of blood, because *Dracula* includes little information about little Quincey Harker, the one character in whom Stoker might have examined heredity. Furthermore, Lucy's four blood transfusions fail to counter Dracula's influence, although she does observe at one point that she feels Arthur's presence warm about her after the first transfusion. That Stoker nonetheless spent so much time focusing on those transfusions suggests that the science was important to him.

For Lucy's first transfusion (from Arthur), Stoker has Van Helsing administer a narcotic to her and notes, "Then with swiftness, but with absolute method, Van Helsing performed the operation" (160). Her second (from Seward) is equally vague—"As he spoke, he was dipping into his bag and producing the instruments for transfusion" (165)—and so are the third (from Van Helsing) and the fourth (from Quincey Morris). Stoker mentions instruments but doesn't describe exactly what kind of apparatus Van Helsing uses for the transfusions. Stoker was familiar enough with transfusions to note that Van Helsing does not "defribinate" the blood (remove the clotting material).

Although transfusions didn't become a safe form of treatment until 1909 when the Austrian-American immunologist Karl Landsteiner established the existence of different blood types, successful human blood transfusions were performed during the nineteenth century. A Guy's Hospital surgeon named James Blundel is credited with performing the first successful human transfusion in 1818 and with using a syringe to transfer blood directly from donor to patient, a practice that continued until 1914, at which time it became possible to store blood. Richard Quain's *Dictionary of Medicine* (1882) includes an article on blood transfusion written by Marcus Beck, an assistant surgeon at University College Hospital, an article that raises the question of whether to defibrinate blood for transfusions.[4] Stoker, who often consulted his brothers Thornley and George about medical matters, could have easily learned about blood transfusions from them. He was certainly familiar with various medical paraphernalia, because Seward and Van Helsing are seen at various points in the novel using scalpels, hypodermic needles, surgical saws, and a trephining instrument. In fact, Seward on several occasions mentions his mentor's medical bag "in which were many instruments and drugs... the equipment of a professor of the healing craft" (157).

That all their medical attention prolongs Lucy's life but is ultimately powerless to save her suggests to me that Stoker was aware of the limitations of science, a field that was rapidly gaining social and political power along with greater proficiency at the end of the nineteenth century. That he also recognized the growing importance of science as a discipline is evidenced in the fact that *Dracula* includes two physicians as main characters as well as a number of other characters who are influenced by a scientific line of inquiry.

The two physicians are Seward and Van Helsing, and Seward certainly begins the novel full of optimism about what science can accomplish:

> Men sneered at vivisection, and yet look at its results to-day! Why not advance science in its most difficult and vital aspect— the knowledge of the brain? Had I even the secret of one such mind ... I might advance my own branch of science to a pitch compared with which Burdon-Sanderson's physiology or Ferrier's brain-knowledge would be as nothing. (95)

He ends by consistently questioning his own sanity and the sanity of his companions although he never threatens to leave the group and never reports any breach of scientific ethics to the appropriate authorities even though Renfield refers to Seward as a "medico-jurist" (295), a term that suggests Seward's familiarity with the law. Despite his knowledge of law, however, Seward never questions Van Helsing's decision to avoid an investigation of Mrs. Westenra's death. Furthermore, his decision to mutilate Lucy's body stems more from emotional response than from a desire to collect scientific evidence:

> When Lucy ... saw us she drew back with an angry snarl, such as a cat gives when taken unawares; then her eyes ranged over us. Lucy's eyes in form and colour; but Lucy's eyes unclean and full of hell-fire, instead of the pure, gentle orbs we knew. At that moment the remnant of my love passed into hate and loathing; had she then to be killed, I could have done it with savage delight. (257)

Indeed, Seward describes the death and subsequent mutilation of Lucy in almost graphic detail.

Of course, Seward is influenced by Dr. Van Helsing, his friend and former teacher, who produces convincing visual evidence of Lucy's transformation and who later convinces all his followers to help him destroy Dracula:

> Even had we not the proof of our own unhappy experience, the teachings and the records of the past give proof enough for sane peoples. I admit that at the first I was sceptic. Were it not that through long years I have train myself to keep an open mind, I could not have believe until such time as that fact thunder on my ear. (286–87)

He adds that his proof might not satisfy a typical scientist, however: "A year ago which of us would have received such a possibility, in the midst of our scientific, sceptical, matter-of-fact nineteenth century" (289). Thus, Stoker presents Van Helsing as a scientist who is nonetheless willing to question the truth associated with science, to question science and to trust traditional wisdom rather than test out his theories. Van Helsing is a unique combination of the scientist and the magician, a scientist who, according to Troy Boone,[5] proposes a science "that validates reason but does not deprivilege the supernatural."[6] Van Helsing seems on most occasions to be the wise old ruler of a group of neophytes as well as a man well-versed in a number of disciplines, including science. There are times, however, when Stoker presents Van Helsing's limitations, including the King Laugh scene and the scene in which his casual comment causes Mina pain: " 'Do you forget,' he said, with actually a smile, 'that last night he banqueted heavily, and will sleep late?' " (351). In addition to these moments of crass behavior, Van Helsing also seems incapable of going beyond certain conventional notions, including the view that women are weak and, therefore, require protection. Such ideas on both race and gender were reinforced by the science of Stoker's day, however, as scientists measured skulls and weighed brains to determine the inferiority of both women and people of color.

For the Blood Is the Life: Dracula *and Victorian Science*

My concerns with Van Helsing's limitations are reinforced by the fact that Stoker occasionally suggests that science is tainted. Renfield, for example, is shown to be a kind of scientist manqué, according to Seward, whose reference to the notebook in which Renfield keeps facts and figures suggests that his patient is recording his experiments. One must question the validity of Renfield's science, however, as he begins with a theorem that is impossible to prove, the idea that he can prolong his life indefinitely by drinking the blood of other living creatures.

Dracula, too, is a kind of scientist. Van Helsing notes that Dracula had been in life an alchemist, which was "the highest development of the science-knowledge of his time," that there was "no branch of knowledge of his time that he not essay," and that he is "experimenting, and doing it well" (360). Van Helsing's references to Dracula's experiments are reinforced by the fact that Dracula labels his earth boxes as 50 "cases of common earth, to be used for experimental purposes" (275). Dracula fails as a scientist too, although for an entirely different reason—he lacks experimental data. In fact, Van Helsing and his followers are able to track Dracula down because Mina observes that Dracula, when faced with a difficulty, "has to seek resource in habit" (403) instead of experimenting until he finds the best solution to a problem.

Although she is never identified as a scientist, possibly because science remained a largely male endeavor at the time Stoker was writing, Mina Harker has one of the best scientific minds in the novel. Unlike Van Helsing, she is rarely dominated by prejudicial views, and she is, moreover, scrupulous about making certain that their evidence is accurate. In fact, Case attributes Dracula's defeat to Mina's "collecting, collating and interpreting information" to determine his "whereabouts, his limitations, his mental character, and his future plans, reducing him from an otherworldly embodiment of all that threatens rationality and social order to a predictable, and, thence, defeatable, 'criminal type.' "[7] Glover also privileges scientific investigation in *Dracula*, noting that science represents "the accumulation and rigorous testing of evidence" and thus ultimately "provides the key to the novel's construction," which consists of a "master discourse" capable of ordering and organizing the "disparate empirical knowledges and variously inflected voices contributed by a succession of narrator-witnesses."[8] The problem is that the scientists are rarely as disinterested as Glover suggests.

Another problem that *Dracula* reveals is that science quickly moves from the desire to understand the world to the desire to control and manipulate it. As Auerbach explains it, the brief scene in which Jonathan Harker notices Dracula's hands resembles the attempts of nineteenth-century scientists to classify their world:

> Hitherto I had noticed the backs of his hands ... and they had seemed rather white and fine; but seeing them now close to me, I could not but notice that they were rather coarse—broad, with squat fingers. Strange to say, there were hairs in the centre of the palm. The nails were long and fine, and cut to a sharp point. (25)

Commenting that Dracula is "fine (aristocratic) in dim light, coarse (animal) when he comes close,"[9] Auerbach moves from Harker's difficulty in classifying Dracula to looking at how questions of taxonomy plagued scientists throughout the nineteenth century:

> The nineteenth-century development Hypothesis, most famously demonstrated in Darwin's revelations of humanity's animal origins, revised Victorian faith in humanism.... Throughout the century, guardians of powerful institutions affirmed their shaky humanity by cataloging and thus controlling animals as Van Helsing does Dracula.[10]

Once they are classified as monstrous aberrations, Lucy, Dracula, and Dracula's women companions are comparatively easy for Van Helsing and his followers to destroy.

Harriet Ritvo, in *The Animal Estate: The English and Other Creatures in the Victorian Age*, looks at the relationship between humans and animals in nineteenth-century England and argues that the scientific desire to classify animals leads to the scientists' desire for control:

For the Blood Is the Life: Dracula and Victorian Science

> At the beginning of this period people perceived themselves to be at the mercy of natural forces; at the end, science and engineering had begun to make much of nature more vulnerable to human control. . . . animals could represent the power of nature, and thus as it became less threatening, so did they. On the pragmatic level advances in such fields as stockbreeding, veterinary science, and weapons technology made actual animals easier to manage. Nowhere were these developments more striking than in England.[11]

Ritvo looks carefully at all aspects of the relationship between human beings and animals during the nineteenth century, but her analysis of the development of the nineteenth-century zoological garden is especially relevant to *Dracula*, a novel that features one important scene in a zoo and also looks closely at the relationship between animals and humans:

> Maintaining exotic animals in captivity was a compelling symbol of human power. Transporting them safely . . . and figuring out how to keep them alive were triumphs of human skill and intelligence over the contrary dictates of nature; access to their native territories symbolized English power and prestige. . . . But for some people caged wild animals presented a further challenge. . . . the ultimate goal was domestication . . . as a crowning metaphorical demonstration of human ascendancy. Most of those involved in organized efforts to domesticate exotic animals were either scientists with a professional interest in illustrating the power of human intellect over nature, or magnates and officials with a social or political interest in emphasizing their dominion over other people. If the rhetoric of public zoos engaged . . . national pride, that of acclimatization and domestication expressed the . . . concerns of the elite audience that [Stamford] Raffles had envisioned when he planned the Zoological Society of London.[12]

Ritvo's conclusions are especially evident in the scene at the zoo, in the experiences that the well-traveled Quincey Morris describes with wolves and with vampire bats, and also in the fact that the English hunters trust in their weapons to overcome animal adversaries.

Thomas Bilder, the keeper from the Zoological Gardens, is apparently not a scientist, although his reference to acquiring several wolves from Jamrach, an animal dealer, reveals Stoker's awareness of the trade in exotic animals. Moreover, Bilder clearly sees his job in terms of control over the animals, because he admits to the reporter for *The Pall Mall Gazette* that he shows off for wealthy visitors by hitting the wolves, lions, and tigers. Although the interview reveals his genuine fondness for the animals in his charge, it also shows that he is in control.

Control is also evident in the weapons that the young Englishmen choose to battle foes other than Dracula. Quincey Morris notes, for example, that Winchester rifles will protect them from wolves:

> I understand that the Count comes from a wolf country. . . . I propose that we add Winchesters to our armament. I have a kind of belief in a Winchester when there is any trouble of that sort around. Do you remember Art, when we had the pack after us at Tobolsk? (383)

Even the terriers that Arthur brings along when the group explores Carfax Abbey are a kind of weapon against the rats that Dracula summons and are thus one more way of demonstrating human superiority over the natural world.

That superiority is also demonstrated by the fact that Dracula and the other vampires are generally classified in terms of their animal behaviors. Harker observes that the blonde vampire at Dracula's castle "actually licked her lips like an animal" (52), and Lucy Westenra's animalistic behavior horrifies Dr. Seward:

> . . . she drew back with an angry snarl, such as a cat gives when taken unawares. . . . With a careless motion, she flung to the ground . . . the child. . . growling over it as a dog growls over a bone. (257)

Whereas the female vampires alternate between bestial and seductive behavior, Dracula himself is almost always presented in animal terms. For example, he clearly identifies with the wolves, noting to Harker:

For the Blood Is the Life: Dracula *and Victorian Science*

"Listen to them—the children of the night. What music they make" (26). Confronting Dracula in his Piccadilly House, Seward compares him to several predatory animals:

> There was something so panther-like in the movement—something so unhuman, that it seemed to sober us all from the shock of his coming... As the Count saw us, a horrible sort of snarl passed over his face, showing the eye-teeth long and pointed; but the evil smile as quickly passed into a cold stare of lion-like disdain. (363–64)

Although these scenes merely compare Dracula to various animals, Van Helsing suggests that Dracula is literally an animal:

> He can transform himself to wolf, as we gather from the ship arrival in Whitby, when he tear open the dog; he can be as bat, as Madam Mina saw him on the window at Whitby, and as friend John saw him fly from this so near house, and as my friend Quincey saw him at the window of Miss Lucy.... He can see in the dark—no small power this, in a world which is one half shut from the light. (289–90)

Finally, whereas most of the animals that Van Helsing mentions are those that would have been construed as noble during the nineteenth century, Jonathan Harker also imagines Dracula as reptilian, crawling down the castle wall, "just as a lizard moves along a wall." Harker then asks, "What manner of man is this, or what manner of creature is it in the semblance of man?" (48). Classifying Dracula as something other than human solves a number of problems, for it makes him easier to hunt down and kill.

Of course, the scientific desire to classify individuals moves from animal populations to human beings as the century progresses, and the same motives that lead naturalists early in the century to bring back exotic species for zoos, museums, and other kinds of scientific collections led social scientists to classify various human populations. Two fields of social science that have particular relevance to our understanding of *Dracula* are anthropology and criminology.

Nineteenth-century anthropology was particularly interested in examining racial characteristics. Joseph Bristow observes, in *Empire Boys: Adventures in a Man's World*, that the same impulse that leads biologists to collect and study exotic animal specimens also motivates a variety of social scientists to collect and study exotic human specimens. Bristow then goes on to argue that these scientific studies actually provide evidence to support various prejudices:

> By mid century, Africans were almost uniformly referred to as "Niger's." A matter of decades later, with pictures of narrow foreheads and ape-like features impressed upon the European mind, earlier prejudices were scientifically legitimated.[13]

Transylvania is not Africa, certainly, but it is clear that Stoker was often thinking along racial lines when he depicted vampires in *Dracula*, a subject that is covered in greater detail in chapter 5. For our purposes here, it is important only to note the extent to which Stoker used nineteenth-century science to condemn his vampires. Not only do they resemble animals, but they also resemble the primitive peoples that were being studied in various scientific fields.

The scientific desire to classify various exotic types also caused social scientists to study people back home as well and eventually led to a variety of social programs designed to control people who deviated too much from the norm. Glover notes specifically that the fear of atavism influenced social policy at the fin de siècle period. Intellectuals at various points on the political spectrum were influenced by the "fear of a slide back down the evolutionary chain," and "the idea of sterilizing the unfit or at least of preventing their reproduction" was commonplace during the 1890s.[14] The English characters often reveal their fear that the vampires will reproduce. Harker admits that he is driven mad by the thought that Dracula will "create a new and ever-widening circle of semi-demons to batten on the helpless" (67). In other words, Harker fears that Dracula will leave his demonic offspring in London. Thinking of Mina, though, Harker later comes to understand that vampires can use love to reproduce as well as violence: "if we find out that Mina must be a vampire in the end, then she shall not go into that unknown and terrible land alone. I suppose it is thus that in old times one vampire meant many. . . . so the holiest love was the recruiting sergeant for their ghastly ranks" (353–54). Van Helsing is even more specific about preventing vampires from reproducing. For example, he argues that "we have this day to hunt out all his lairs and *sterilise* them" (348, my emphasis). His language with regard to Dracula and the other vampires thus resembles the language of those social scientists who wished to prevent unfit individuals from reproducing.

Of course, Dracula and the other vampires are often compared to criminals, a subject that has been thoroughly explored, most specifically by Troy Boone, Ernest Fontana, David Glover, Salli J. Kline, and Daniel Pick. All these writers point to Stoker's familiarity with Max Nordau's *Degeneration* (1893), which established the relationship between genius and degeneracy, and with Cesare Lombroso, who is often considered the father of modern criminology. Lombroso originally claimed that criminal behavior could be explained in terms of evolutionary atavism, as Kline effectively explains, noting that Lombroso's major contribution to nineteenth-century thought was to apply Darwin's theory of atavism to human beings. Thus "the so-called 'born criminal' " was a "sudden throwback to a phylogenetically older form of life." Kline concludes that the Swiss medical historian Ackerknecht "makes the significant observation that Lombroso's theory ... amounts to a definition of the world's criminal population as a 'sort of surviving primordial race.' "[15] Lombroso's emphasis on the notable physical traits of criminals also explains why Stoker spent so much time studying the appearance of vampires. The physical details reveal that vampires are atavistic beings who display the deliberate cruelty of primitive human beings as well as the ferocious instincts of animals.

That Stoker was aware of both Nordau and Lombroso is clearly evident in *Dracula*, for Mina reveals her familiarity with their thought: "The Count is a criminal and of criminal type. Nordau and Lombroso would so classify him, and *quâ* criminal he is of imperfectly formed mind" (403). In fact, her knowledge of criminal behavior provides her with the information they need to track Dracula: "Then, as he is criminal he is selfish; and as his intellect is small and his action is based on selfishness, he confines himself to one purpose. That purpose is remorseless" (404).

Finally, because this chapter examines the science in *Dracula*, it is important to note that, whereas Van Helsing generally attempts to explain the existence of vampires in terms of biology and anthropology, he at one point accounts for their existence in terms of geology and chemistry:

> The very place, where he have been alive, Un-Dead for all these centuries, is full of strangeness of the geologic and chemical world. There are deep caverns and fissures that reach none know whither. There have been volcanoes, some of whose openings still send out waters of strange properties, and gases that kill or make to vivify. Doubtless, there is something magnetic or electric in some of these combinations of occult forces which work for physical life in strange way; and in himself were from the first some great qualities. (378)

Stoker once again returned to geology in his final novel, *The Lair of the White Worm*, when he attempted to explain the presence of a dinosaur-like creature in England. In *Dracula*, however, he was more indebted to biology and anthropology.

Whether he used biology or anthropology, however, Stoker was consistent about identifying the vampire as a member of an inferior species and about using scientific means to destroy this dangerous interloper. As Van Helsing explains to his followers, "We have on our side power of combination—a power denied to the vampire kind; we have sources of science" (288). Thus, it would appear that even religious artifacts such as the Host and the crucifix fall under the general rubric of science because they have been tested and found efficacious.

Stoker was obviously very interested in science, and *Dracula* concludes with an apparent victory of the scientists over Dracula and the other vampires. In spite of their victory, however, *Dracula* leaves the reader with some gnawing questions about science and the ways it is used. According to Feimer and Heilbronn, *Dracula* reveals the limitations of both science and scientists. Heilbronn observes that three nineteenth-century novels (*Dracula*, *Frankenstein*, and *Dr. Jekyll and*

Mr. Hyde) introduce two themes that are increasingly evident in contemporary science fiction: "the helplessness of science in the face of supernatural forces, and the potential of science to go too far . . . and become an instrument of destruction" and adds that the themes are even more relevant today: "These themes have become more pressing in the nuclear age, as fears about mass destruction and doubts about the value of technology have become widespread."[16] Heilbronn is obviously thinking of the fact that the physicians in these novels cannot use their science to cure their patients, and she may also be thinking of the English characters' willingness to annihilate anything that they cannot control. Feimer has a somewhat different idea about the limitations of science in *Dracula*, observing that *Dracula* "summoned ancient histories of horror and age-old beliefs in occult phenomena to mount a challenge to the rising arrogance of reason, science, and psychiatry." Feimer adds: "What Stoker's novel objects to most is the insistence of the mainstream of modern thought on the reality of a quantifiable universe that excludes all possibility of the objective existence of the occult."[17] Feimer concludes that *Dracula* warns readers against "the dangers of rational skepticism and of too heavy a reliance on science and the quantifiable to explain the universe" (168). He would thus agree with Hamlet's warning to his scholarly friend that "there are more things in heaven and earth than are dreamt of in your philosophy." These unspeakable, irrational things include vampires.

Both Feimer and Heilbronn caution readers against accepting without question the apparently happy ending of *Dracula*, and I want to remind readers that the novel confronts us with several other thorny issues about science. Not only are both Renfield and Dracula presented as scientists manqué, but the science in the novel is often used to justify acts of almost unbearable cruelty. These facts, combined with the novel's ineffectual science, suggest that Stoker may have been less confident about the direction that science might take than is implied by the apparently happy ending. Ambivalence about the future is certainly consistent with Stoker's general worldview, because his novels often attempt to preserve the best part of traditional life and to combine those traditions with better ways of doing things. Dr. Van Helsing seems to combine both the best of the traditional world with the most advanced science, yet even he is sometimes wrong, especially when his scientific judgment causes him to ignore other sources of information. *Dracula* thus suggests to me at least that any single-minded approach—whether that approach is scientific or religious or something entirely different—is likely to be misguided and harmful.

9

Typewriters, Trains, and Telegrams: The Technology of *Dracula*

Reading *Dracula* reveals that Stoker and his characters are clearly fascinated with the modern technological developments that made the lives of middle-class Londoners easier at the end of the nineteenth century. This chapter focuses on the technology in *Dracula*, which I define broadly as practical or applied science and therefore distinguish, albeit somewhat arbitrarily, from the pure science that I examine in the previous chapter. Looking at technology in the novel, I agree with Anne McWhir who observes, in "Pollution and Redemption in *Dracula*," that the "world of the novel is busily, even obsessively, modern"[1] and uses as evidence Van Helsing's trips across the channel, Mina's typing, and Seward's use of a phonograph.

Other examples of technology in the novel include Winchester repeating rifles, telegrams, trains, blood transfusions, Kodak cameras, steam-powered boats, electric lamps, and the London Underground. It is almost as though Dracula's modern opponents assemble a whole arsenal of technological materials to use in their battle against him.

The reliance on these technological devices is consistent with the fact that Dracula's opponents all embody very late Victorian virtues and characteristics while he remains a creature from the past, a stranger both in London and in the nineteenth century despite his professed desire to learn about England so he can fit in with his new surroundings. If it weren't for Stoker's open ending to the novel (is Dracula truly destroyed when Harker stabs him, or does he merely dissolve into mist so that he can return once again?), I might simply describe *Dracula* as a tribute to technology. *Dracula*, however, is rarely as simple as it initially appears.

Several critics interpret the technology in a positive fashion. Ronald D. Morrison observes that "tension between gothic, supernatural elements and the scientific advances of the late Victorian age strongly pervades" *Dracula* and adds that Dracula's opponents "display an enormous confidence in technology and their own scientific training" even though they also rely "on such non-scientific aids as crucifixes, wooden stakes, garlic, and all the other vampire-hunting paraphernalia."[2] Regenia Gagnier[3] focuses even more specifically on the triumph of information, science, and technology:

> England casts the net that catches the Count and defeats the forces of myth and superstition by enlisting an international network of scientists and scholars, reflecting contemporary methods of "research" and the progress of professionalisation.... The institutional collaboration of business, law and government reflects the late-Victorian consolidation of management techniques with technology.[4]

Whereas McWhir, Morrison, and Gagnier focus on the positive aspects of technology, other critics who also observe the presence of modern technology in the novel argue that *Dracula* is hardly a paean to technology. For example, John Greenaway notes that although *Dracula* is filled with examples of Victorian technology, "Dracula is finally dispatched with exotic weapons of American and Indian frontiers: Quincey's Bowie knife and Harker's Ghurka knife."[5] Boone, who comments on Harker's enthusiasm for technology at the novel's opening, observes that Harker quickly learns that technology is useless against Dracula, an argument with which McWhir agrees. McWhir notes furthermore that "the technology the book makes so much of is less important in defeating Dracula than sacramental magic"[6] and also makes an important observation about technology: that certain characters don't know how to use it. As an illustration, she cites the telegram that Van Helsing sends to Seward, which is delayed because he doesn't include an adequate address. Van Helsing's carelessness leads to the night of terror that causes the death of Lucy's mother and the death of Lucy herself several days later.[7] I might add that, even though Harker finds Dracula reading an English Bradshaw's Guide (a list of timetables for the English railway system) and is comforted by this familiar detail, Dracula seems to be uncomfortable with modern technology, preferring horses and sailing ships to more modern means of transportation. In fact, Van Helsing and Dracula are both similarly handicapped by being unfamiliar with technology, which is somewhat surprising because Dr. Seward describes Van Helsing as "one of the most advanced scientists of his day" (147) and because Dracula's library is filled with books, magazines, and newspapers by which he means to familiarize himself with English life and customs. The question in *Dracula*, therefore, seems to revolve around the significance of technology rather than with its mere presence.

Stoker himself was personally familiar with much of the technology that he described in *Dracula*. In *Hollywood Gothic: The Tangled Web of Dracula from Novel to Stage to Screen*, David J. Skal includes a typed page from Stoker's manuscript of *Dracula* to which Stoker had added handwritten changes. Belford also notes that Stoker heard Tennyson read "on a recorded cylinder" and "borrowed the device for Dr. Seward, who used it to record case histories."[8] In addition, Belford also mentions that Stoker originally intended to make Quincey Morris an inventor[9] rather than an adventurer, and Quincey remains fascinated with gadgets. Finally, as business manager for the Lyceum Theatre, Stoker spent much of his time arranging travel plans for the touring company and was therefore familiar with travel by train and ship as well as with advances in lighting and other technological developments that were important to the theater.

Looking at Stoker's other novels provides additional examples of his interest in technology, including the automobile in *Lady Athlyne*, the airplane in *The Lady of the Shroud*, and explosives in both

The Lair of the White Worm and *The Mystery of the Sea*. The mere presence of modern technology in his novels doesn't necessarily argue for Stoker's enthusiasm for it, however, because Stoker's novels are also filled with material from history and archaeology, an interest that is clearly evident in *The Jewel of Seven Stars* and *The Lair of the White Worm* as well as in *Dracula*.

What is particularly interesting is that so many of Stoker's horror novels juxtapose modern technological developments with monstrous creatures from the past whose power threatens to overwhelm the present: vampires in *Dracula*, a mummy in *The Jewel of Seven Stars*, and a dinosaur in *The Lair of the White Worm*. Furthermore, in each of these novels, Stoker's heroes are familiar with modern technology and often use it to battle these ancient monsters. (*The Jewel of Seven Stars* is an exception in that most of the protagonists do not see the mummy of Queen Tera as a threat and therefore do not attempt to destroy her. Failing to recognize her as a monster, they are destroyed by her instead.) In *Dracula*, the heroes use both modern means of transportation (trains, the London Underground, Holmwood's steam launch) and modern methods of communication (telegrams, newspapers, telephones, typewriters, and shorthand, which neither Dracula nor Van Helsing can read). Traveling at breakneck speed to Dracula's castle, Dr. Seward regrets having to resort to a more primitive form of communication: "How I miss my phonograph! To write diary with a pen is irksome to me; but Van Helsing says I must" (396). Mina Harker similarly appreciates the technological developments that make modern communication more quick and efficient: "I feel so grateful to the man who invented the 'Traveller's' typewriter" (414).

On the other hand, the heroes occasionally find that their modern technological conveniences let them down. Harker notes that trains are sometimes slow, especially in the East. An accident to Holmwood's steam launch prevents him and Harker from overtaking the more primitive boat on which Dracula's last earth box is located. Many technological developments, including blood transfusions, are powerless against Dracula while other modern medicines are positively dangerous. Dr. Seward, for example, warns against the dangers of taking chloral hydrate but later prescribes it for Mina, a decision that leaves her more vulnerable to Dracula's attack. Furthermore, even though they frequently rely on modern technological developments, Dracula's opponents are often concerned that the past may be more powerful than their technology. Nowhere is this power more evident than in the scene just before Jonathan Harker meets the three vampire-women in Dracula's castle, the three being literal embodiments of the past that Harker both fears and admires. Harker refers to his diary, which he keeps in shorthand as "nineteenth century up-to-date with a vengeance. And yet, unless my senses deceive me, the old centuries had, and have, powers of their own which mere 'modernity' cannot kill" (49–50). Harker later realizes, when he locates Dracula's final resting place, exactly how helpless he is against such supernatural beings: "I wished I had a gun or some lethal weapon, that I might destroy him; but I fear that no weapon wrought alone by man's hand would have any effect on him" (64). Finding themselves confronted with something new and frightening, Stoker's characters ultimately discover that they must rely equally on new technology and on ancient superstition, such as the garlic and the wooden stake that they use against the vampire.

Stoker's heroes discover that they must use both modern technology and ancient knowledge to battle Dracula. Furthermore, *Dracula* constantly reminds readers that modern technology exists alongside older forms of knowledge and in the presence of the ruins of ancient civilizations. These ruins include the remnants of Whitby Abbey that Mina notes in her diary and the most significant relic of all, Dracula's castle, which Harker describes as "a vast ruined castle, from whose tall black windows came no ray of light, and whose broken battlements showed a jagged line against the moonlit sky" (19). At the conclusion, little remains but memories and the castle, which "stood as before, reared high above a waste of desolation" (444).

The presence of ruins in *Dracula* and the juxtaposition of up-to-date technology with ancient wisdom brings me to a related issue, Stoker's interest in the past, an interest that pervades *Dracula* as well as Stoker's other novels.

As an educated and cosmopolitan resident of London, Stoker would have known about the ruins of classical civilizations, the Near East, and Egypt that filled the British Museum even if his interest in archaeological ruins hadn't been reinforced by his friendships with Oscar Wilde's father, Sir William Wilde, and Sir Richard Burton.[10] Both Wilde and Burton had participated in archaeological explorations of Egypt, and Burton, who is better known today for his explorations of central Africa and his translation of the *Arabian Nights,* had published his findings in 1879. Even without the personal connections, however, Stoker could have learned about the past from a variety of sources that were readily available to most literate English. Indeed in *Men among the Mammoths: Victorian Science and the Discovery of Human Prehistory*,[11] A. Bowdoin Van Riper comments on the pervasive nineteenth-century interest in archaeology and observes that many of the same people who were interested in the present were also interested in archaeology:

> In 1851, the year that the Crystal Palace opened and tens of thousands flocked to London to gape at the wonders of the modern age, Britons were also fascinated by their island's distant past. The rapid proliferation of archaeological societies reflected this growing interest.... Of the two national and forty-one county archaeological societies founded in England between 1830 and 1880, half were established ... between 1840 and 1855. The new societies made archaeology a nationwide enterprise for the first time in Britain. By the late 1850s, it was an established scientific discipline with a large, enthusiastic community of researchers.... Three national journals and a dozen or more local ones gave archaeologists a forum for their ideas, and the annual summer meetings of the British Archaeological Association and the Archaeological Institute drew large crowds.[12]

Thus interest in the past seems to have arisen at precisely the same time as the rise of appreciation for technological developments. Certainly, Stoker's amateur archeologists, Sir Nathaniel de Salis in *The Lair of the White Worm* and Edward Trelawney in *The Jewel of Seven Stars*, are almost as enthusiastic about technological developments as they are about the past.

Interest in archaeology may even be connected to the interest in modern technology, as Christopher Chippindale suggests in " 'Social Archaeology' in the Nineteenth Century: Is it Right to Look for Modern Ideas in Old Places?"[13] Chippendale connects the interest in archaeology with the awareness of technological sophistication and notes that Sir John Lubbock, the key figure in Victorian British archaeology and the author of *Pre-historic Times, as Illustrated by Ancient Remains and the Manners and Customs of Modern Savages* (1865), was a good friend of such eminent scientists as Charles Darwin, Thomas Henry Huxley, and Herbert Spencer. Chippendale even implies that Lubbock's book links the interest in modern technology with attention to the past:

> Despite the inconsistencies of savage virtue and vice, Lubbock sees a pattern of progress from savages—slaves to their wants, neither noble nor free—to civilized persons whose lives are spent, *thanks to printing*, in communion with the greatest minds.... Ever the rational optimist, Lubbock ends with a peek at the future and sees how mankind always progresses towards less pain and more happiness as science abolishes the evil that comes from ignorance and sin.[14]

Lubbock's view about progress seems remarkably similar to the view held by both Stoker's English characters and Dr. Van Helsing.

In fact, thanks to modern print communications, Dracula's opponents are able to learn about the historical Dracula and to use that knowledge to fight him. Van Helsing learns Dracula's history from his friend Arminius of Buda-Pesth University, and Mina later studies history to discover where Dracula is hiding:

> His past is a clue, and the one page of it that we know—and that from his own lips—tells that once before.... he went back to his own country from the land he had tried to invade, and thence, without losing purpose, prepared himself for a new effort. He came again better equipped for his work; and won. So he came to London to invade a new land. He was beaten, and when all hope of success was lost, and his existence in danger, he fled back over the sea to his home; just as formerly he had fled back over the Danube from Turkey-land. (403)

Thus, Dracula's English opponents combine their knowledge of the historical past with modern technology in the battle to conquer Dracula. They also insist that this knowledge makes them superior to their opponent.

The belief in historical progress was a characteristically nineteenth-century belief partially brought about, I suspect, by the simultaneous development of technology and the discovery of archaeological materials that made people during that period acutely aware of their differences from the individuals who had produced such artifacts. Certainly, nineteenth-century thinkers practically mandated the understanding of history. J. W. Burrow, in *A Liberal Descent: Victorian Historians and the English Past*, argues that Victorian historians, from Burke onward, had "held that political wisdom, and the identity of a society, and hence in some measure the appropriate conduct of its affairs, are found essentially in its history."[15] In *Reversing the Conquest: History and Myth in 19th-Century British Literature*, Clare A. Simmons also examines the nineteenth-century fascination with the past:

> Michel Foucault has remarked that the sense of history as a fact-controlling discipline was largely a product of the nineteenth century. Hayden White has gone further in suggesting that from the mid-nineteenth century, the historical task had been seen as the discovery of "what happened." After having established a factual foundation, the historian is entitled to be "dissertative" and to offer an interpretation of those facts.[16]

Modris Eksteins, in "History and Degeneration: Of Birds and Cages,"[17] connects the new interest in history with Darwinian science:

> Darwin revealed that nature was hardly the static, mechanical reality which the *philosophes* and the Hegelians considered it but a dynamic reality which too had a history; and this revelation suggested that historical scholarship might hold the key to the development of a total view of the universe including both spirit and nature.[18]

Nineteenth-century thinkers had an acute interest in the past, an interest that is evidenced by the collections in the British Museum, by the rise of archaeology as a discipline, and by the development of history as a field of professional study.

Because Stoker was a writer, however, his interest in history might have also come from more purely literary sources. In addition to Sir Walter Scott, who practically invented the historical novel, almost every nineteenth-century writer chose to focus on historical materials at least once. Among the most familiar examples are Thomas Carlyle's *Past and Present* and Charles Dickens's *A Tale of Two Cities*. Simmons, however, cites several examples that are especially relevant to *Dracula*—Bulwer-Lytton's *Harold*, W. Harrison Ainsworth's *The Tower of London*, and Charles Kingsley's *Hereward the Wake, the Last of the English*. According to Simmons, these novelists "placed historically documented figures (that is, figures not invented by the novelist) at the center of their stories."[19] Stoker uses a similar strategy in *Dracula* and *The Jewel of Seven Stars*, although he adds an element of fantasy by collapsing time periods and by introducing historical figures to his own present.

Although Stoker was a prolific reader, no specific evidence indicates that he was familiar with any of the works mentioned in the previous paragraph. There is evidence of his familiarity with the one work that Simmons cites as the "final, and most influential, product of this phase," Tennyson's *Becket* (1879), which "was performed, apparently to some acclaim, in Britain and the United States. Henry Irving's 1893 adaptation gained popularity in its own right."[20] Not only was Stoker familiar with Irving's adaptation of *Becket*, but the timing was important, because Stoker was working on *Dracula* at the same time that Irving was preparing *Becket* for the stage.

Thinking about the nineteenth-century interest in history brings me, in a very circuitous way, back to *Dracula* and ultimately to the questions about technology that are posed in its pages. Does *Dracula* celebrate the technological developments that were taking place at the time Stoker was writing, developments that he incorporated into his novel? Or is *Dracula* a paean to the power of the past which "mere 'modernity' cannot kill"?

Stoker, in fact, looked at both the power of technology and the power of tradition. His university training in mathematics and science and his personal fascination with technological developments made him particularly well situated to feature technology in his fiction. Because Stoker was also born into a traditional world and clearly felt pulled in the direction of tradition, he abandoned his initial impulse to make Quincey Morris an inventor and chose instead to focus on characters who combine both knowledge of technology and knowledge of the past. Reluctant to abandon either the power and mystery of the past or the technological developments of the present, Stoker wrote a novel that leaves readers with several important questions: Is Dracula destroyed by the proponents of modern technology? Or will this powerful figure from the past return once again to haunt and terrorize the modern world even though he is one of the only characters in the novel who seems incapable of using modern technology?

Once again, Stoker seems to have discovered something that remains important to subsequent generations of readers. Even as we acquire more sophisticated technology in the forms of film, television, and computers and use these technological advances to interpret Stoker's novel, we continue to be fascinated with the past that was Vlad Dracula and his brides and to shudder with both terror and desire as we see elements of these monsters in ourselves. The fascination of *Dracula* is especially evident on the World Wide Web, which includes material on various vampire films and stage adaptations, electronic versions of Stoker's novel, biographical material on Stoker, games based on the novel, virtual tours of both Whitby and of Dracula's homeland, model kits of various characters, and costumes. Here too, the power and mystery of *Dracula* have clearly been appropriated by yet another technological form.

As readers of Stoker's novel, we desire both technology and mystery, the physical ease that we associate with progress and the romance that we associate with past ages. Stoker, born into a more traditional world than we twentieth-century readers will ever know, obviously understood what it meant to be pulled in two directions also, toward the past and toward the future.

10

The Comedy of Class:
Blood, Drunkenness, and Hard Work

Recent studies of *Dracula* are full of excellent material on Stoker's treatment of gender and race, but there is very little information—either recent or old—about class. Considering the importance of class in the nineteenth century (including the fact that the various Reform Bills extended political power to members of the middle class and finally to the working class as well; the fact that simultaneous changes in the economic structure had also taken financial power away from the aristocracy and given it to the middle classes; and the fact that so many people in the nineteenth century were concerned about this social fluidity), it would be a mistake to ignore class when reading anything written in the nineteenth century.

Moreover, although the nineteenth-century preoccupation with class should motivate readers of any nineteenth-century work to examine class issues, Stoker's novel is obvious in its treatment of class. Not only does Dracula's move to England from Transylvania result in the confrontation of a primitive or medieval world with the modern world and also in the confrontation of the past with the present, but Dracula himself is a titled aristocrat, one of only two aristocrats in a novel whose main characters are solidly middle class. (The number of aristocrats escalates to three if readers agree with me that Renfield is also a member of the aristocracy; the question of Renfield's class is addressed later in this chapter.)

In addition, *Dracula* includes a number of working-class individuals and demonstrates that the values and beliefs of these individuals are quite different from those held by the middle-class protagonists. In terms of sheer theater, Stoker's treatment of the English working class (and the superstitious Romanian peasants as well) can be seen as comic relief, a brief respite in the midst of an otherwise terrifying novel, and an example of what Stoker had learned all those evenings at the Lyceum Theater. As this chapter demonstrates, however, Stoker's treatment of class does more than provide comic relief. Indeed, class is connected to other important issues in the novel, especially to issues of race and gender, but also to issues of science.

As with so much of what Stoker wrote, his examination of class reveals him as a transitional figure. Born into an age which has close ties to the past and its traditions, he occasionally looked nostalgically to that past. At the same time, Stoker was himself solidly middle class and ideologically supportive of the values and beliefs associated with the rising middle class. *Dracula,* in its treatment of class, is a Janus-like work that looks, as it does with questions of gender and sexuality and with the rise of science and technology, both to the past and to the future.

There is no doubt that Stoker saw Dracula as an embodiment of the past. It is therefore appropriate that Dracula represents the aristocracy, a group that in the nineteenth century is losing its traditional power, as David Punter observes of one possible model for Dracula, Polidori's Lord Ruthven:

> He is dead yet not dead, as the power of the aristocracy in the early nineteenth century was dead and not dead; he requires blood because blood is the business of an aristocracy, the blood of warfare and the blood of the family.[1]

Choosing to travel to England, Dracula describes himself by the title of Count. Even when picking an alias—"Count de Ville, who effected the purchase himself paying the purchase money in notes 'over the counter' " (326)—he chooses to present himself as an aristocrat. Besides reinforcing his status as an aristocrat, however, the name "Count de Ville" and the Piccadilly location also identify Dracula as a particular kind of exploitative aristocrat. Kline explains that the realistic fiction of the period depicts Piccadilly as the part of London in which "fallen servant girls and adulterous wives turned away from home eventually landed—and ... the place where lechers from ... the West End came in hopes of picking them up" and adds that "the Count de Ville is a London stereotype, the man about town in the Nineties, the lecherous dandy, the barloafer."[2] Unfamiliar with Piccadilly as a place notorious for sexual assignations, contemporary readers may not recognize that Stoker's choice of an alias for Dracula connects him with the aristocratic sexual predators of his day.

It is easier to see the link between aristocracy and power, because Dracula usually identifies himself in terms of mastery. Early in the novel, he boasts of a distinguished lineage that he can trace all the way back to Attila and tells Harker that he has been long accustomed to the mastery that comes with his privileged position: "Here I am noble; I am *boyar*; the common people know me, and I am master.... I have been so long master that I would be master still—or at least that none other should be master of me" (28, Stoker's emphasis). Dracula also reveals that he believes this mastery is the result of his natural superiority: "Bah! what good are peasants without a leader? Where ends the war without a brain and heart to conduct it?" (42). Although Dracula's pride in his military prowess makes Harker uncomfortable initially, Harker and the other men are willing to recognize the appropriateness of such behavior in the warlike past. In fact, Van Helsing praises the deeds of the historical Dracula when he informs the little group about their adversary:

> He must, indeed, have been that Voivode Dracula who won his name against the Turk.... If it be so, then was he no common man; for *in that time*, and *for centuries after*, he was spoken of as the cleverest and the most cunning, as well as the bravest of the sons of the "land beyond the forest." (291, my emphasis)

The italicized passages suggest that Van Helsing sees Dracula as something of an anachronism, a being whose time has passed, an aristocrat and a warlord in a largely peaceful and democratic age. Celebrating the past achievements of such an aristocratic leader, Van Helsing nonetheless implies that the skills that he celebrates are no longer much in demand except perhaps in frontier regions such as the American West or Africa.

If aristocratic leadership is no longer valued in democratic England, other characteristics of the aristocracy have become positively repellent. One of these characteristics is the personal relationship between the aristocrat and the people around him. In his personal dealings with others, it is clear that Dracula sees himself as the owner of people rather than as their leader. Caught in the Harkers' bedroom, he is quick to taunt his male opponents with his power over them: "Your girls that you all love are mine already; and through them you and others shall yet be mine—my creatures, to do my bidding and to be my jackals when I want to feed" (365). Thus his relationship to Lucy appears to be the equivalent of the medieval droit du seigneur, a custom in which the new bride was deflowered by the lord of the manor rather than by the bridegroom. Furthermore, Dracula's relationship with Mina (and the presence of his "harem" in Transylvania) suggests his unwillingness to share women even with their lawful husbands.

Dracula's own words, as recorded by his opponents, indicate that he sees himself as a master of all that he surveys, as a leader of men, as a husband to all the women, and as the ruler with the power of life and death over all his subjects.

His opponents, on the other hand, regard these aristocratic attitudes as hopelessly out of date. Van Helsing, for example, praises both Dracula's past heroism and his present attempts to learn new ways but nonetheless describes him as childish and ineffectual:

> With the child-brain that was to him he have long since conceive the idea of coming to a great city.... He find out the place of all the world most of promise for him. Then he deliberately set himself down to prepare for the task. He find in patience just how is his strength, and what are his powers. He study new tongues. He

learn new social life; new environment of old ways, the politic,
the law, the finance, the science, the habit of a new land and a
new people who have come to be since he was. (379–80)

Despite all Dracula's attempts to learn about the present—including
the books, magazines, and newspapers that Harker finds in his library—Stoker presents Dracula as a creature whose attitudes lock him
in the past. For example, Mina notes that, when faced with a difficult
problem, Dracula is forced to retreat to past behaviors rather than attempt to discover new solutions: "Thus, in a difficulty he has to seek
resource in habit" (403). She adds that his aristocratic habits can also
be used against him, for his belief in his own natural superiority causes
him to think only of saving himself when faced with difficulty: Because "his intellect is small and his action is based on selfishness, he
confines himself to one purpose.... As he fled back over the Danube,
leaving his forces to be cut to pieces, so now he is intent on being safe,
careless of all" (404). This behavior is very different from that of his
opponents, who are both willing to sacrifice themselves to help others
and eager to join forces to fight against him.

In terms of class, Dracula's opponents are solidly middle class
with the exception of Arthur Holmwood, whose father's death early
in the novel makes him Lord Godalming. These opponents consist of
doctors, lawyers, teachers, and businessmen, professional people who
gained political power only during the nineteenth century. Arthur
Holmwood blends in with this solid middle-class group except in one
scene in which the distinctive accoutrements of the aristocracy are
presented as a distinct liability. When the group plans to break into
Dracula's Piccadilly house, Arthur offers to have "horses and carriages
where they will be most convenient." Quincey replies that those
"snappy carriages with its heraldic adornments ... would attract too
much attention for our purposes" (350) and proposes that the group
substitute cabs, a decidedly nonaristocratic method of transportation.

Finally, although the connection of the vampire to excess sexuality is covered in greater detail in chapter 6, it is appropriate to mention here that the middle class often associated both the aristocracy
and the working class with unrestrained sexuality. Regarding sexual

purity as an important goal, the middle class therefore condemned members of other classes for sexual overindulgence.

Arthur Holmwood is an aristocrat by birth, but his sexual reticence connects him with the middle class. Faced with Lucy's increasing sexuality before her death, he dutifully obeys when Van Helsing warns him not to kiss her. Later, when she attempts to embrace him in the cemetery, he once again turns away from temptation. These scenes suggest that, unlike Dracula, Arthur Holmwood is an aristocrat who shares the values of the rising middle class rather than those of the class into which he is born. He is good friends with both the solidly middle-class Dr. Seward and with the rough-and-tumble Quincey Morris, and he learns to love both the middle-class Harkers and Dr. Van Helsing as well. In fact, Lucy Westenra, when courted by Holmwood, Morris, and Seward, seems to recognize no differences among them in terms of class. Her letter to Mina suggests that she chooses Arthur based exclusively on her love for him rather than because of any privileges that his rank might confer on her.

Arthur seems equally unaware of any power or distinction that his family background might accord him. Although he inherits property from both his father and from Mrs. Westenra, he seems to have no more power than other wealthy people in the novel, including Morris and the nouveau riche Harkers. Moreover, he chooses to join forces with his middle-class friends rather than insist on leading them in the quest to destroy Dracula.

Stoker's positive treatment of the aristocratic Holmwood suggests that Dracula's character is emblematic of a corrupt and moribund aristocracy. On the other hand, because Stoker's treatment of class is as complex as his treatment of science or gender, it is also important to see that Stoker connects Dracula with other individuals who are out of touch with the ways of the modern world, most significantly with the Gypsies and Slovaks of his own country and with members of the English working class. Thus, Dracula, apparently the archetypal aristocrat, is also linked in numerous significant ways both with what remains of the rural peasantry in Transylvania and with the urban working class in England. The connection is perhaps appropriate, for the aristocracy had once provided protection and employment for the peasantry whereas the trades and professions had always been independent.

In general, Stoker is condescending toward his working-class characters, presenting them as drunkards and cowards, occasionally even as thieves. After tracking down the workers who had unloaded the boxes of earth at Carfax, Jonathan Harker notes sarcastically that these laborers found it very "dry work" and bemoaned the fact that no gentleman showed any "sort of appreciation of their efforts in a liquid form; another put in a rider that the thirst then generated was such that even the time which had elapsed had not completely allayed it" (275). Still on the trail of Dracula's boxes of earth, Harker observes that another workman, Thomas Snelling, finds that the "very prospect of beer which my expected coming had opened to him had proved too much, and he had begun too early on his expected debauch" (313).

That Stoker associates English laborers with their drinking habits might seem to be nothing more than either comic relief or Stoker's own class prejudice except that the repeated emphasis on drinking in this novel connects the workers with Dracula. Like them, Dracula is also a drinker, a creature totally controlled by his need for blood. Furthermore, just as the English laborers sleep off the ill effects of their liquid refreshments, Dracula is occasionally observed in his coffin, sleeping off the effects of *his* overindulgence:

> There lay the Count.... the mouth was redder than ever, for on the lips were gouts of fresh blood, which trickled from the corners of the mouth and ran over the chin and neck. Even the deep, burning eyes seemed set amongst swollen flesh, for the lids and pouches underneath were bloated. It seemed as if the whole awful creature were simply gorged with blood; he lay like a filthy leech, exhausted with his repletion. (67)

The hard-working and temperate Harker is clearly disgusted by such overindulgence.

In addition to being drunkards, members of the working class often behave as cowards. When faced with the need to give Lucy a blood transfusion, Van Helsing is hesitant even to ask her servants: "I fear to trust those women, even if they would have courage to submit"

(188). Similarly the interview in *The Pall Mall Gazette* with the keeper in the zoological gardens suggests that working-class individuals are both cruel and cowardly. The interviewer quotes Thomas Bilder, the keeper, who admits that he shows off for visitors by hitting the wild animals or scratching their ears but only when the animals are safely behind bars or sated with food:

> 'Ittin' of them over the 'ead with a pole is one way; scratchin' of their hears is another, when gents as is flush wants a bit of a show-orf to their gals. I don't so much mind the fust—the 'ittin' with a pole afore I chucks in their dinner; but I waits till they've 'ad their sherry and kawffee, so to speak, afore I tries on with the ear-scratchin'. (176)

The anonymous interviewer seems to include the colorful Cockney accent merely for the amusement of his middle-class readers, and Stoker's use of dialect does establish Bilder as a member of a different group. The emphasis on his cowardice, however, also connects Bilder with other cowardly working-class characters. Indeed, Stoker portrays his working-class characters as cowards, the exceptions being the brave captains of the *Demeter* and of the *Czarina Catherine*.

Finally, working-class individuals are presented as motivated by the desire for material gain. One supposedly loyal serving woman is actually a thief who steals the gold cross from Lucy's dead body, and numerous other working-class characters are willing to accept bribes either of money or drink without thinking of potential consequences.

Because of his emphasis on the physical natures of both his aristocratic characters and his working-class characters, Stoker seems to suggest that both are creatures of the body who are primarily concerned with material gain and sensuous pleasures. Furthermore, although Dracula sees himself as a superior member of a superior class, Stoker often connects him to the working class in obvious ways. He is, for example, often involved with what are considered working-class occupations. While still in Transylvania, Dracula "works" as a coachman, a cook, a chambermaid, and a valet. (The presence of gold in his castle suggests that he also digs up the buried treasure that he, in the guise of coachman, locates on St. George's Eve.) In fact, because Dracula is so proficient at these tasks, it takes Jonathan Harker several days to realize that the castle is deserted. Coming quietly to his own room, he finds Dracula making the bed and comments: "This was odd, but only confirmed what I had all along thought—that there were no servants in the house" (38).

In England, Dracula adds another menial occupation to his résumé of skills—that of laborer. Indeed, Sam Bloxam, the laborer who helps him unload the boxes of earth at Dracula's Piccadilly house, comments admiringly on Dracula's physical prowess: "He 'elped me to lift the boxes and put them in the dray. Curse me, but he was the strongest chap I ever struck, an' him a old feller... one that thin you would think he couldn't throw a shadder" (316).

That Dracula is alternately connected with both the aristocracy and with the peasantry is yet one more indication of how complex the class issue was during the nineteenth century. A further example that reveals how difficult class was to establish occurs in the early chapters, when Jonathan Harker is exploring Dracula's castle. Finding himself in the women's area of the castle, Harker is drifting off to sleep when he is awakened by "three young women, *ladies* by their dress and manner" (51, my emphasis). Harker's initial designation suggests that the three are ladies, members of the aristocracy or at least the upper middle classes. He is subsequently horrified when their behavior becomes distinctly unladylike. Instead of waiting for an appropriate introduction, they accost him as though they were common streetwalkers plying their wares. Temporarily intrigued by their sexual behavior, Harker seems almost more disconcerted by his inability to put them in the appropriate class. Because they defy his attempts to categorize them, Harker concludes that they aren't women at all: "I am alone in the castle with those awful women. Faugh! Mina is a woman, and there is nought in common. They are devils of the Pit!" (69).

Despite these ambiguous links between the aristocracy and the working class, Stoker's presentation of class in *Dracula* suggests that his middle-class characters are solid, hard working, and progressive and that both the aristocracy and the working classes have been arrested in the past. This discussion of class would not be complete, however, without examining the enigmatic Renfield, a figure whose madness would seem to put him outside any normal discussion of class.

What exactly is Renfield? Dr. Seward introduces him with a brief description: "R. M. Renfield, aetat 59.—Sanguine temperament; great physical strength" (80). The physical characteristics that Seward observes provide at least a superficial link with Dracula. Both are physically strong; both are described as selfish; and both are apparently devourers of life. Indeed, Renfield's desire to ingest more lives is what attracts him to Dracula in the first place. Because Stoker reveals surprisingly little about Renfield's social background in the early chapters, however, the reader is likely to view Renfield only as an interesting patient or as a plot device for getting Dracula into Seward's hospital, where he can attack Mina.

One interesting scene suggests, however, that more social commentary is involved in Renfield's character. That scene is the one in which a surprisingly sane Renfield begs Seward to release him from the asylum. Although the reader later discovers that Renfield has been shocked into sanity by the realization that Dracula has drunk the blood of Mina Harker, the reader immediately understands that the scene reveals Renfield's disenchantment with the creature he had earlier welcomed as his master. Moreover, thinking of the scene along class lines may also suggest that Renfield has become disenchanted with the powerful aristocracy and that he now believes in the rightness of democratic collaboration. Whatever the reason, from this scene until his death, Renfield identifies with the group of middle-class professionals who oppose Dracula rather than with the aristocratic Dracula.

Shaking hands with the men who come to visit him, Renfield speaks to each of them in turn. On a superficial level, the scene reveals Renfield's awareness of social protocol. Speaking to Quincey Morris of the Monroe Doctrine, he points to the future power of the United States once it abandons isolationist policies. He speaks to Van Helsing and reveals that he is familiar with the doctor's scientific research. Most important in terms of this discussion of class, though, is his response to Arthur Holmwood, to whom he says that he had "the honour of seconding your father at the Windham" and recognizes the senior Godalming as "the inventor of a burnt rum punch, much patronised on Derby night" (295). This brief scene does not provide conclusive proof that Renfield is an aristocrat, but it combines with the earlier scene in which he meets Mina Harker to reveal that he is an educated man as well as a man who had moved in the same social circles as the elder Holmwood. Apparently a gentleman, although not necessarily an aristocrat, Renfield is moreover in his current state an idle one, linked to Dracula in that both are parasites rather than productive members of their society. His decision to save Mina from Dracula and to join with Dracula's middle-class opponents suggests a shift in his class allegiance.

Unlike the idle aristocracy, which can choose to rest on past laurels, and unlike the shiftless working class, which would rather drink, fight, and loaf, Stoker's middle-class protagonists are singularly hard working. Harker is apparently an impoverished orphan, although his hard work has already helped him rise, while still a very young man, from clerk in a solicitor's office to solicitor to full partner and owner of the firm. The efforts that led to this meteoric rise are evident in his journal. Not only is he eager to go to Transylvania to complete the deal because his employer requests him to do so, but he uses the opportunity to refine his business skills. For example, he practices shorthand and uses every opportunity available to learn about his chosen profession, the law. Later, when Mina has been tainted by the vampire's baptism of blood, he puts all his legal skills to good service tracking down the monster who had corrupted her.

Although it is dangerous to read too much of Stoker's biography into the novel, a number of similarities between Harker and his creator should be noted. Not only are both familiar with the law, but both share a singular sense of duty. Kline examines Stoker's years as a civil servant, a decidedly middle-class occupation, and describes Stoker as a man who "took his civic obligations seriously, a man obsessed with a sense of duty." As evidence, she cites his first published lengthy work, *The Duties of Clerks of Petty Sessions in Ireland*, which she describes as "a treatise on duty" and notes that it was "later adopted by the Irish government as an official set of guidelines for the less naturally ambitious men in their employ."[3] A stern sense of duty and the willingness to work hard are certainly characteristics that Stoker shares with his middle-class characters.

If Jonathan Harker is presented as a man of duty and hard work, his wife Mina is perhaps even busier; in addition to her job as an assistant schoolmistress, a job that, she informs Lucy, keeps her "overwhelmed with work" (71), she practices shorthand and typewriting skills, keeps a journal to sharpen her memory, and learns train schedules so that she can help Jonathan with his work after their marriage. As a married woman, she continues to work on her secretarial skills, manages their household, and also coordinates the intellectual discoveries of all Dracula's opponents. In fact, she seems to hold the group together even before Dracula's attack unifies them in their battle to save her from the vampirish taint.

Seward is another character whose hard work and dedication to his profession identify him as middle class. A physician and the director of a London hospital for the insane, he keeps a thorough clinical diary that reveals both his attention to medical details and his concern with his patients. If the notes on all his patients are as comprehensive as those on Lucy and Renfield, he is conscientious almost to a fault. Indeed, Stoker presents Seward as such a dedicated professional that he can find solace in work when Lucy rejects his proposal of marriage: "Oh, Lucy, Lucy, I cannot be angry with you, nor can I be angry with my friend whose happiness is yours; but I must only wait on hopeless and work. Work! work!" (96). In fact, he can easily be identified with the civilized man who channels repressed passion into activity.

Yet another middle-class professional who has turned personal disappointment into professional achievement is Abraham Van Helsing. Stoker has Van Helsing reveal that he had lost a child and that his wife is mad. Despite these personal sorrows, however, Van Helsing has earned three doctoral degrees (in medicine, philosophy, and literature) as well as a degree in law. Furthermore, Seward describes his old mentor to Arthur as "a philosopher and a metaphysician, and one of the most advanced scientists of his day" (147). A man of exceptional training and ability, Van Helsing maintains a schedule that would be arduous even for a much younger man, as he travels back and forth between London and Amsterdam to discover the ailment that has afflicted Lucy Westenra and later as he learns more about Dracula. Nonetheless, while Van Helsing is clearly an exceptional human being, he has made his mark in fields that, during the nineteenth century, would have identified him as solidly middle class.

The last of Dracula's opponents, Quincey Morris, seems to be middle class as well, although he is, like Renfield, difficult to categorize. An American, Morris would therefore never be considered aristocratic, although he apparently comes from a wealthy family and had, in his youth, been accustomed to travel with Seward and Holmwood. He has traveled all over the world and is known mostly for his familiarity with weapons and horses. Above all, he seems to be a type of American adventurer. (For a discussion of the racial and ethnic attributes of Morris's character, see chapter 5.) Not usually talkative, Morris admits his lack of polish to Mina: "I'm only a rough fellow, who hasn't, perhaps, lived as a man should to win such a distinction, but I swear to you by all that I hold sacred and dear that, should the time ever come, I shall not flinch from the duty that you have set us" (391). Reinforcing his lack of sophistication is Mina's later observation that he is the only member of the group who does not speak any foreign language. Thus Morris seems to partake of all classes, having the physical prowess of the aristocracy and the working class and the moral values of the middle class.

Stoker's most recent biographer, Barbara Belford, notes that Stoker made certain changes in Morris's character, changes that provide an interesting footnote to our discussion of class. Although *Dracula* presents him as an adventurer, he was originally "an American inventor called Brutus M. Moris."[4] The change in Morris's character suggests that Stoker may have originally wished to include Morris with the other middle-class characters but later chose to emphasize his adventurous American character.

Moreover, the changes that Stoker makes in Morris's character cause him to resemble Dracula more than he resembles the other middle-class characters. He is characterized by the bowie knife that he carries and by the impulsive habit of shooting at shadows, even in the city. Looking at him as a warrior and a frontiersman enables readers to see his resemblance to Dracula and also suggests why he and Dracula are killed at the conclusion. In a society that is oriented to a scientific and legalistic future rather than to a heroic past, both Dracula and Morris are anachronisms. Leatherdale suggests this connection when he notes that "Texas was viewed by many Americans as a marginal region almost at the edge of civilization" (129). Looking at Texas along these lines suggests a similarity with Dracula's home, Transylvania or "the Land Beyond the Forest." Perhaps Stoker is suggesting that the future would have no place for such remnants of the past.

There is no question that the middle class is victorious in *Dracula* or that values associated with either the aristocracy or the peasantry have been effaced. Returning seven years later to the scene of their battle with Dracula, Jonathan Harker specifically mentions the virtues of self-sacrifice and chastity, observing that "the happiness of some of us since then is, we think, well worth the pain we endured" and adding that "Godalming and Seward are both happily married" (444). As Garret Stewart argues, the conclusion proves that Dracula, "deracinated aristocrat and nosferatu both," is defeated "by the collective entrepreneurial energies of the professional bourgeois cabal—or cartel—marshaled against him."[5] Kline also comments on the middle-class ideology pervasive in *Dracula*, noting that Stoker's "views were those of the day, views that were held not only by the Philistine middle classes but which were vigorously propagated in the natural, social and legal sciences by men who were considered to be the voice of reason itself."[6] Greenway also insists that the conclusion emphasizes the status quo at the time that Stoker was writing:

> The bland, asexual tableau at the end, when the characters return to Transylvania for old times' sake, officially announces the triumph of the Victorian conventions of rationality and progress. . . . The men, emblems of the establishment as scientist, solicitor, and aristocrat, have become husbands and providers while Mina, who has the best mind of the lot, has become Jonathan's secretary.[7]

All these commentators agree that *Dracula* celebrates the rise of the nineteenth-century bourgeois.

It is impossible to deny that the conclusion of *Dracula* celebrates the rising middle class or that Stoker shares some of the smug moral superiority of his middle-class characters. On the other hand, to see *Dracula* simply as the triumph of bourgeois ideology is to ignore much of its power and to deny its rich depiction of both the aristocracy and the working classes. The Harkers and their middle-class associates may destroy the vampire, but they nonetheless return to the site of their victory over him. Furthermore, they preserve the record of their battle with him secure in a safe even though they acknowledge that few would believe their tale.

There is one more dimension to their story, however, for although his characters conceal their strange story, Stoker shares it with the world. It is almost as though he was thereby implying that the rise of the middle class will never totally eliminate the past from which it sprung or the conflicts that helped it to define itself. Despite its apparent effacement at the conclusion, the power of the heroic past radiates through *Dracula*.

The power of that past is evident in one change that Belford notes between the manuscript and the novel:

> Stoker destroyed the castle after Dracula's death, obliterating all vampiric traces. But someone, at the last moment, deleted 195 words including ... "From where we stood it seemed as though the one fierce volcano burst had satisfied the need of nature and that the castle and the structure of the hill had sunk again into the void."[8]

Belford doesn't indicate who chose to delete this brief passage. Omitting this passage, however, leaves a visible emblem of the past as a constant reminder of its power. That the dying Dracula is also surrounded by his loyal retainers while his castle remains standing long after the battle is over are indications that the aristocratic past, though moribund, is not totally dead even in the forward-looking nineteenth century.

Notes and References

3. Critical Reception

1. For an overview of the criticism of Stoker's works, see Carol A. Senf, ed., *The Critical Response to Bram Stoker* (Westport, Conn.: Greenwood Press, 1993).

2. Barbara Belford, *Bram Stoker: A Biography of the Author of Dracula* (New York: Alfred A. Knopf, 1996), 260–61.

3. David Glover, *Vampires, Mummies, and Liberals: Bram Stoker and the Politics of Popular Fiction* (London and Durham: Duke University Press, 1996), 3.

4. Cited by Belford, 274–75.

5. "Review of *Dracula*," *Spectator* 79 (31 July 1897): 151.

6. "Review of *Dracula*," *Bookman* 12 (August 1897): 129.

7. "Review of *Dracula*," *Athenaeum* 109 (26 June 1897): 835.

8. *Spectator*, 151.

9. The following critical studies examine science/social science in the novel: Joel N. Feimer, "Bram Stoker's *Dracula*: The Challenge of the Occult to Science, Reason, and Psychiatry," in *Contours of the Fantastic: Selected Essays from the Eighth International Conference on the Fantastic in the Arts*, ed. Michele K. Langford (New York: Greenwood, 1990), 165–171; Ernest Fontana, "Lombroso's Criminal Man and Stoker's *Dracula*," *Victorian Newsletter* 42 (1972): 20–22; John Greenway, "Seward's Folly: *Dracula* as a Critique of 'Normal Science,' " *Stanford Literature Review* 3 (1986): 213–30; Lisa M. Heilbronn, "Natural Man, Unnatural Science: Rejection of Science in Recent Science Fiction and Fantasy Film," in *Contours of the Fantastic: Selected Essays from the Eighth International Conference on the Fantastic in the Arts*, ed. Michele K. Langford (New York: Greenwood, 1990), 113–19; Rosemary Jann, "Saved by Science? The Mixed Messages of Stoker's *Dracula*," *Texas Studies in Literature and Language* 31 (Summer 1989): 273–87; Daniel Pick, "Terrors of the Night: *Dracula* and 'Degeneration' in the Late Nineteenth Century," *Critical Quarterly* 30 (Winter 1988): 71–87.

10. "Review of *Dracula*," *Punch* (26 June 1897).

11. For a good bibliography of films, see Raymond T. McNally, *Dracula Was a Woman* (New York: McGraw-Hill, 1983), 234–44.

12. Harry Ludlam, *A Biography of Dracula: The Life Story of Bram Stoker* (London: Foulsham, 1962).

13. Bacil F. Kirtley, "Dracula, the Monastic Chronicles and Slavic Folklore," *Midwestern Folklore* 6 (1956): 133–39.

14. Richard Wasson, "The Politics of Dracula," *English Literature in Transition* 9 (1966): 24–27.

15. Charles Osborne, ed., *The Bram Stoker Bedside Companion* (London: Quartet, 1972).

16. Raymond T. MacNally and Radu Florescu, *In Search of Dracula* (Greenwich, Conn.: New York Graphic Society, 1972).

17. Leonard Wolf, *A Dream of Dracula* (Boston: Little, Brown, 1972).

18. Christopher Bentley, "The Monster in the Bedroom: Sexual Symbolism in Bram Stoker's *Dracula*," *Literature and Psychology* 22 (1972): 27–34.

19. Joseph S. Bierman, "*Dracula*: Prolonged Childhood Illness and the Oral Triad," *American Imago* 29 (1972): 186–98.

20. Jean Gattegno, "Folie, Croyance et Fantastique dans 'Dracula,' " *Litterature* 8 (December 1972).

21. Royce MacGillivray, " 'Dracula': Bram Stoker's Spoiled Masterpiece," *Queen's Quarterly* 79 (1972): 518–27.

22. Daniel Farson, *The Man Who Wrote Dracula: A Biography of Bram Stoker* (New York: St. Martin's, 1975).

23. Phyllis A. Roth, *Bram Stoker* (Boston: Twayne, 1982).

24. Clive Leatherdale, *Dracula: The Novel and the Legend* (Wellingborough, Northamptonshire: Aquarian, 1985).

25. Stephen D. Arata, "The Occidental Tourist: *Dracula* and the Anxiety of Reverse Colonization," *Victorian Studies* 33 (Summer 1990): 621–45.

26. Patrick Brantlinger, "Imperial Gothic: Atavism and the Occult in the British Adventure Novel, 1880–1914," *ELT* 28 (1985): 243–52.

27. Burton Hatlen, "The Return of the Repressed/Oppressed in Bram Stoker's *Dracula*," *Minnesota Review* 15 (1980): 80–97.

28. Alison Case, "Tasting the Original Apple: Gender and the Struggle for Narrative Authority in *Dracula*," *Narrative* I (October 1993): 223–43; Ronald D. Morrison, "Reading Barthes and Reading *Dracula*: Between Work and Text," *Kentucky Philological Review* 9 (1994): 23–28.

29. Stephanie Demetrakopoulos, "Feminism, Sex Role Exchanges, and Other Subliminal Fantasies in Bram Stoker's *Dracula*," *Frontiers* (1977):

Notes and References

104–13; Gail B. Griffin, " 'Your Girls That You All Love are Mine': *Dracula* and the Victorian Male Sexual Imagination," *International Journal of Women's Studies* 3 (1980): 454–65; Cyndy Hendershot, "Vampire and Replicant: The One-Sex Body in a Two-Sex World," *Science-Fiction Studies* 22 (1995): 373–98.

30. Christopher Craft, " 'Kiss Me with Those Red Lips': Gender and Inversion in Bram Stoker's *Dracula*," *Representations* 8 (1984): 107–33; Talia Schaffer, " 'A Wilde Desire Took Me': The Homoerotic History of *Dracula*," *ELH* 61 (1994): 381–425.

31. John Greenway, "Seward's Folly: *Dracula* as a Critique of 'Normal Science,' " *Stanford Literature Review* 3 (1986): 213–30; Rosemary Jann, "Saved by Science? The Mixed Messages of Stoker's *Dracula*," *Texas Studies in Literature and Language* 31 (Summer 1989): 273–87; Jennifer Wicke, "Vampiric Typewriting: Dracula and Its Media," *ELH* 59 (1992): 467–93.

4. Narrative Strategy in *Dracula*: Journals, Newspapers, and Diaries

1. This telegram is found on page 82 in *The Essential Dracula*, ed. Leonard Wolf (New York: Plume, 1993). All subsequent references to *Dracula* are from this edition and are included parenthetically in the text.

2. Salli J. Kline, *The Degeneration of Women: Bram Stoker's Dracula as Allegorical Criticism of the Fin de Siècle* (CMZ-Verlag: Rheinbach-Merzbach, 1992).

3. Kline, 25.

4. Kline, 275.

5. Leatherdale, 116.

6. Case, 228.

7. Wicke, 485.

8. Case, 229–30.

9. Case, 229.

10. Case, 230.

11. Case, 233.

5. Traveling to Transylvania: Race, Space, and the British Empire

1. Arata, 84–85.

2. Cannon Schmitt, "Mother Dracula: Orientalism, Degeneration, and Anglo-Irish National Subjectivity at the Fin de Siècle," in *Irishness and (Post) Modernism*, ed. John S. Rickard (Lewisburg, Pa.: Bucknell University Press,1994), 25–43.

3. Schmitt, 30.

4. Wasson, 23.

5. Belford, 264.

6. Arata, 87.

7. Judith Halberstam, "Technologies of Monstrosity: Bram Stoker's *Dracula*," *Victorian Studies* (Spring 1993): 333–52.

8. Halberstam, 337.

9. Halberstam, 335.

10. Arata, 91.

11. Robert Tracy, "Loving You All Ways: Vamps, Vampires, Necrophiles, and Necrofilles in Nineteenth-Century Fiction," in *Sex and Death in Victorian Literature*, ed. Regina Barreca (Bloomington: Indiana University Press, 1990), 32–59.

12. Tracy, 38.

13. Schmitt, 26.

14. Elaine Showalter, *Sexual Anarchy: Gender and Culture at the Fin de Siècle* (New York: Viking, 1990), 5.

15. Joseph Bristow, *Empire Boys: Adventures in a Man's World* (London: HarperCollins Academic, 1991).

16. Bristow, 130.

17. Brantlinger, 245.

18. Brantlinger, 247.

19. Brantlinger, 245.

20. Glover, 23.

21. Belford, 77.

22. Bristow, 131.

23. Anne McWhir, "Pollution and Redemption in *Dracula*," *Modern Language Studies* 17 (1987): 31–40.

24. McWhir, 38.

25. Judith Halberstam, *Skin Shows: Gothic Horror and the Technology of Monsters* (Durham, N.C.: Duke University Press, 1995), 86.

26. Bram Stoker, *Personal Reminiscences of Henry Irving*, vol. 1 (1906; reprint, Westport, Conn.: Greenwood Press, 1970), 358–59.

6. Those Monstrous Women: A Discussion of Gender in *Dracula*

1. Belford, 5.

2. Belford, 7.

3. Deborah Epstein Nord, *Walking the Victorian Streets: Women, Representation, and the City* (Ithaca: Cornell University Press, 1995).

4. Nord, 9–10.
5. Belford, 265.
6. Wicke, 481.
7. Kline, 111–12.
8. Kline, 113.
9. Kline, 260.
10. Glover, 97.
11. Karl Beckson, *London in the 1890s: A Cultural History* (New York: W. W. Norton, 1992), 129.
12. Glover, 109.
13. Anne Williams, *Art of Darkness: A Poetics of Gothic* (Chicago: University of Chicago Press, 1995), 123.
14. Maurice Richardson, "The Psychoanalysis of Ghost Stories," *Twentieth Century* 166 (1959): 419–31.
15. Richardson, 427.
16. Nina Auerbach, *Our Vampires, Ourselves* (Chicago: University of Chicago Press, 1995), 7.
17. Auerbach, 83.
18. Auerbach, 83.
19. Schaffer, 381.
20. Schaffer, 398.
21. Schaffer, 409.
22. Schaffer, 406.
23. Showalter, 3.

7. This Way Madness Lies: Nightmares, Schizophrenia, Religion, and Confusion about Boundaries

1. Wolf quotes from an advertising brochure in a footnote on page 284.
2. Belford, 244.
3. John 3:24–29.
4. Williams, 118.
5. Feimer, 165–71.
6. Feimer, 166.
7. Garret Stewart, " 'Count Me In': *Dracula*, Hypnotic Participation, and the Late-Victorian Gothic of Reading," *LIT* 5 (1994): 1–18.
8. Stewart, 2.
9. Glover, 15.

10. Kline, 9.

11. Hendershot, 376.

8. For the Blood Is the Life: *Dracula* and Victorian Science

1. Belford, 19.

2. Glover, 10.

3. Kline, 181–82.

4. I am indebted to the VICTORIA news group for this information on transfusions and particularly to Bruce Rosen and Lynn Schoch for their expertise.

5. Troy Boone, " 'He Is English and Therefore Adventurous': Politics, Decadence, and *Dracula*," *Studies in the Novel* 25 (Spring 1993), 76–91.

6. Boone, 81.

7. Case, 223.

8. Glover, 63.

9. Auerbach, 88.

10. Auerbach, 91–92.

11. Harriet Ritvo, *The Animal Estate: The English and Other Creatures in the Victorian Age* (Cambridge, Mass: Harvard University Press, 1987), 2–3.

12. Ritvo, 232–34.

13. Bristow, 131.

14. Glover, 65.

15. Kline, 36–37.

16. Heilbronn, 113.

17. Feimer, 165.

9. Typewriters, Trains, and Telegrams: The Technology of *Dracula*

1. McWhir, 31.

2. Morrison, 25.

3. Regenia Gagnier, "Evolution and Information, or Eroticism and Everyday Life, in *Dracula* and Late Victorian Aestheticism," in *Sex and Death in Victorian Literature*, ed. Regina Barreca (Bloomington: Indiana University Press, 1990), 140–57.

4. Gagnier, 149.

5. Senf, 83.

6. McWhir, 33.

7. McWhir, 36.

8. Belford, 232.

9. Belford, 264.

10. That Stoker was familiar with the British Museum reading room is clear from the first chapter of *Dracula,* in which Jonathan Harker observes that he has learned about Transylvania by searching among the books and maps in the British Museum.

11. A. Bowdoin Van Riper, *Men among the Mammoths: Victorian Science and the Discovery of Human Prehistory* (Chicago: University of Chicago Press, 1993).

12. Van Riper, 15.

13. Christopher Chippindale, " 'Social Archaeology' in the Nineteenth Century: Is It Right to Look for Modern Ideas in Old Places?" in *Tracing Archaeology's Past: The Historiography of Archeology,* ed. Andrew L. Christenson (Carbondale: Southern Illinois University Press, 1989), 21–33.

14. Chippendale, 28–29.

15. J. W. Burrow, *A Liberal Descent: Victorian Historians and the English Past* (New York: Cambridge University Press, 1983), 195.

16. Clare A. Simmons, *Reversing the Conquest: History and Myth in 19th-Century British Literature* (New Brunswick: Rutgers University Press, 1990), 13.

17. Modris Eksteins, "History and Degeneration: Of Birds and Cages," in *Degeneration: The Dark Side of Progress,* ed. J. Edward Chamberlin and Sander L. Gilman (New York: Columbia University Press, 1985), 2–23.

18. Eksteins, 5.

19. Simmons, 143.

20. Simmons, 137.

10. The Comedy of Class:
Blood, Drunkenness, and Hard Work

1. David Punter, *The Literature of Terror: A History of Gothic Fictions from 1765 to the Present Day* (London: Longman, 1980).

2. Kline, 192.

3. Kline, 170–71.

4. Belford, 264.

5. Stewart, 9.

6. Kline, 269.

7. Senf, 83.

8. Belford, 267–68.

Selected Bibliography

Primary Works

Dalby, Richard. *Bram Stoker: A Bibliography of First Editions.* London: Dracula Press, 1983. Interesting discussion of various editions of all Stoker works in all languages.

Osborne, Charles, ed. *The Bram Stoker Bedside Companion.* London: Quartet, 1972. Intelligent introduction to collection of Stoker short stories, including "Dracula's Guest."

Stoker, Bram. *Personal Reminiscences of Henry Irving.* 1906. Reprint, Westport, Conn.: Greenwood Press, 1970. Provides Stoker's own voice on his relationship with his employer.

Wolf, Leonard, ed. *The Essential Dracula: The Definitive Annotated Edition of Bram Stoker's Classic Novel.* New York: Penguin, 1975. This edition, which includes copious explanatory notes, was set from the Yale University Library's copy of the second printing of the first edition.

Secondary Works
Books and Parts of Books

Ardis, Ann L. *New Women, New Novels: Feminism and Early Modernism.* New Brunswick: Rutgers, 1990. Scholarly discussion of New Woman novels and their relationship to Modernism.

Auerbach, Nina. *Our Vampires, Ourselves.* Chicago: University of Chicago Press, 1995. Interpretation of vampire motif puts *Dracula* in a literary context.

Selected Bibliography

Beckson, Karl. *London in the 1890s: A Cultural History.* New York: W. W. Norton, 1992. Full scholarly history of the period during which Stoker wrote *Dracula.*

Belford, Barbara. *Bram Stoker: A Biography of the Author of Dracula.* New York: Alfred A. Knopf, 1996. Excellent biography takes advantage of unpublished archival material. Includes numerous illustrations and photographs.

Carter, Margaret L., ed. *Dracula: The Vampire and the Critics.* Ann Arbor: UMI Research Press, 1988. Thoughtful collection of 21 essays includes every conceivable critical approach to the novel as well as a thorough bibliography.

Farson, Daniel. *The Man Who Wrote Dracula: A Biography of Bram Stoker.* New York: St. Martin's, 1975. Biography by Stoker's great-nephew takes advantage of various family anecdotes.

Glover, David. *Vampires, Mummies, and Liberals: Bram Stoker and the Politics of Popular Fiction.* London and Durham: Duke University Press, 1996. Takes cultural studies approach to Stoker's fiction, including *Dracula,* and examines it within its social and historical context.

Halberstam, Judith. *Skin Shows: Gothic Horror and the Technology of Monsters.* Durham: Duke University Press, 1995. Examines anti-Semitism in *Dracula* and also suggests the importance of the gothic in nineteenth-century literature.

Leatherdale, Clive. *Dracula: The Novel and the Legend.* Wellingborough, Northamptonshire: Aquarian, 1985. Provides a critical overview of the novel, including a summary of background materials and various critical approaches. Includes illustrations and bibliography.

Ludlam, Harry. *A Biography of Dracula: The Life Story of Bram Stoker.* London: Foulsham, 1962. First biography of Stoker provides a sort of public record of the events in which Stoker was involved.

Kline, Salli J. *The Degeneration of Women: Bram Stoker's Dracula as Allegorical Criticism of the Fin de Siècle.* CMZ-Verlag: Rheinbach-Merzbach, 1992. Examines various late-nineteenth-century scientific materials concerning women and shows how Stoker wove them into the novel.

MacNally, Raymond T., and Radu Florescu. *In Search of Dracula.* Connecticut: New York Graphic Society, 1972. Traces background material concerning Vlad V of Romania, the Renaissance warlord on whom Stoker is said to have modeled Dracula. Also includes biographical material on Stoker and his work on the novel.

MacNally, Raymond T. *Dracula Was a Woman.* London: Hale, 1984. Examines another historical monster, Elizabeth Bathory, the Blood Countess. Includes excellent bibliography of films.

Punter, David. *The Literature of Terror: A History of Gothic Fictions from 1765 to the Present Day*. London: Longman: 1980.

Roth, Phyllis A. *Bram Stoker*. Boston: Twayne, 1982. Psychoanalytic analysis of Stoker's novels. The only critical study so far to examine all Stoker's novels. It is flawed to the extent that it doesn't take into account the way that many of Stoker's novels have been altered since his death.

Senf, Carol A., ed. *The Critical Response to Bram Stoker*. Westport, Conn.: Greenwood, 1993. Chronological study of critical examinations of Stoker's work. Chapter on *Dracula* suggests how the critical perspective on the novel has changed in the century since it was first published.

Skal, David J. *Hollywood Gothic: The Tangled Web of Dracula from Novel to Stage to Screen*. New York: Norton, 1990. Looks at the various interpretations of *Dracula* but also includes material on Stoker's writing habits.

Williams, Anne. *Art of Darkness: A Poetics of Gothic*. Chicago: University of Chicago Press, 1995. Study of gothic as a way of seeing the world includes an excellent chapter on *Dracula* as a gothic novel.

Wolf, Leonard. *A Dream of Dracula*. Boston: Little, Brown, 1972. Study includes material on *Dracula* and other gothic works, vampires, Stoker, and Stoker's literary circle. Includes photographs.

Articles

Arata, Stephen D. "The Occidental Tourist: *Dracula* and the Anxiety of Reverse Colonization." *Victorian Studies* 33 (Summer 1990): 621–45. Thoroughly documented essay looks at *Dracula* and numerous other late-nineteenth-century works within the context of British imperialism. Helps explain the characters' apprehensions about Dracula's move to London.

Bierman, Joseph S. "*Dracula*: Prolonged Childhood Illness and the Oral Triad." *American Imago* 29 (1972): 186–98. Psychoanalytic study examines *Dracula* and several of Stoker's short stories.

———. "The Genesis and Dating of *Dracula* from Bram Stoker's Working Notes." *Notes and Queries* 24 (1977): 39–41. One of the first studies to examine Stoker's papers. Shows the amount of research that Stoker put into the novel.

Boone, Troy. " 'He Is English and Therefore Adventurous': Politics, Decadence, and *Dracula*." *Studies in the Novel* 25 (Spring 1993): 76–91. Addresses the way that *Dracula* exposes the dangers of failing to question dominant political and scientific beliefs.

Brantlinger, Patrick. "Imperial Gothic: Atavism and the Occult in the British Adventure Novel, 1880–1914," *ELT* 28 (1985): 243–52. Looks at im-

Selected Bibliography

perial Britain's anxiety about atavism as it is revealed in adventure literature, including *Dracula*.

Case, Alison. "Tasting the Original Apple: Gender and the Struggle for Narrative Authority in *Dracula*." *Narrative* I (October 1993): 223–43. Argues that the complex narrative structure of *Dracula* reveals a struggle between Mina and the men for narrative control, a struggle that turns out to involve the proper distribution of masculine and feminine qualities among characters.

Craft, Christopher. " 'Kiss Me with Those Red Lips': Gender and Inversion in Bram Stoker's *Dracula*." *Representations* 8 (1984): 107–33. Examines how *Dracula* confronts various apprehensions about gender at the turn of the century.

Demetrakopoulos, Stephanie. "Feminism, Sex Role Exchanges, and Other Subliminal Fantasies in Bram Stoker's *Dracula*." *Frontiers* (1977): 104–13. Examines Stoker's response to the nineteenth-century feminist movement, especially as Stoker's response is embodied in *Dracula*'s women characters.

Fontana, Ernest. "Lombroso's Criminal Man and Stoker's *Dracula*." *Victorian Newsletter* 42 (1972): 20–22. One of the first studies of Stoker's awareness of nineteenth-century social science.

Greenway, John. "Seward's Folly: *Dracula* as a Critique of 'Normal Science.' " *Stanford Literature Review* 3 (1986): 213–30. Places *Dracula* within the context of Victorian science. Thoroughly documented.

Griffin, Gail B. " 'Your Girls That You All Love Are Mine': *Dracula* and the Victorian Male Sexual Imagination." *International Journal of Women's Studies* 3 (1980): 454–65. Examines Dracula's virtual absence in the novel that bears his name and emphasizes the sexuality of the women characters in the novel.

Hatlen, Burton. "The Return of the Repressed/Oppressed in Bram Stoker's *Dracula*." *Minnesota Review* 15 (1980): 80–97. Marxist examination of the "other" in *Dracula* reads Stoker's fantasy as an examination of the real world.

Hendershot, Cyndy. "Vampire and Replicant: The One-Sex Body in a Two-Sex World." *Science-Fiction Studies* 22 (1995): 373–98. Examines Stoker's concern with the realignment of gender definitions in fin de siècle England and suggests that he introduced the one-sex body as a means of emphasizing the horror and fascination of shifting gender norms.

Jann, Rosemary. "Saved by Science? The Mixed Messages of Stoker's *Dracula*." *Texas Studies in Literature and Language* 31 (Summer 1989): 273–87. Interprets *Dracula* as a text that seems to react against materialist science and its rationalist authority but finally endorses them.

Kirtley, Bacil F. "*Dracula*, the Monastic Chronicles and Slavic Folklore." *Midwestern Folklore* 6 (1956): 133–39. Early scholarly study of *Dracula* examines some of the source materials that Stoker might have consulted to create his vampire count.

MacGillivray, Royce. "'Dracula': Bram Stoker's Spoiled Masterpiece." *Queen's Quarterly* 79 (1972): 518–27. Examines the literary merits and defects of Stoker's novel and argues that only Stoker's weak characterization prevents *Dracula* from being recognized as a masterpiece.

McWhir, Anne. "Pollution and Redemption in *Dracula*." *Modern Language Studies* 17 (1987): 31–40. Examines the complexity of *Dracula* and shows that the crusade against Dracula is a ritual of purification that seems to reestablish clear distinctions between classes and categories. However, because these clear distinctions also break down not far beneath the surface of the novel, "*Dracula* confronts characters and readers alike with the primitive basis of the whole modern, scientific superstructure."

Morrison, Ronald D. "Reading Barthes and Reading *Dracula*: Between Work and Text." *Kentucky Philological Review* 9 (1994): 23–28. Examines the narrative structure of Dracula; suggests that it is a modern work that is independent from traditional, respectable literature and argues that its fragmentary nature is one of the reasons that people "continue to read it with such guilty pleasure."

Review of *Dracula*. *Athenaeum* 109 (26 June 1897): 835.

Review of *Dracula*. *Bookman* 12 (August 1987): 129.

Review of *Dracula*. *Punch* (26 June 1897).

Review of *Dracula*. *Spectator* 79 (31 July 1897): 150.

Schaffer, Talia. " 'A Wilde Desire Took Me': The Homoerotic History of *Dracula*." *ELH* 61 (1994): 381–425. Examines the personal relationship between Stoker and Oscar Wilde.

Senf, Carol A. "*Dracula*: Stoker's Response to the New Woman." *Victorian Studies* 26 (1982): 33–49. Examines Stoker's response to the New Woman novelists of the 1890s.

Wasson, Richard. "The Politics of *Dracula*." *English Literature in Transition* 9 (1966): 24–27. Early scholarly study examines politics in the novel.

Wicke, Jennifer. "Vampiric Typewriting: Dracula and Its Media." *ELH* 59 (1992): 467–93. Examines technology in *Dracula*.

Index

Index

Index

jectivity at the Fin de Siècle,"
36, 39
science, 4; limitations of, 77–80, 86–88
science studies, 15
Scripture, 67–68
Scott, Sir Walter, 97
Separate Spheres, 4, 47
Seward, Dr. John: and blood transfusion, 76; and insanity, 66–67; as middle class character, 104, 110; as narrator, 20–21, 30–31; response to Lucy's transformation, 51, 77–78; as scientist, 77
Showalter, Elaine, *Sexual Anarchy: Gender and Culture at the Fin de Siècle*, 39, 61
shorthand, 93
Skal, David J., *Hollywood Gothic: The Tangled Web of Dracula from Novel to Stage to Screen*, 91
Social Darwinism, 6
Spencer, Herbert, 95
Spectator, The, review of *Dracula*, 12, 13
Stewart, Garret, "'Count Me In': *Dracula*, Hypnotic Participation, and the Late-Victorian Gothic of Reading," 72
Stoker, Abraham (father), xi, xii; professional life of, 3
Stoker, Bram: attitude on duty, 109–10; attitude on working class, 105–7; childhood of, xi, 74–75; college experience, 41; education at Trinity, 75; enthusiasm for technology, 91–92; experience as Inspector of Petty Sessions, 41; interest in past, 93–97, 113; views on changing roles for women, 47; views on race, 41

WORKS: NONFICTION
Duties of Clerks of Petty Sessions in Ireland, The, xii, 41; as treatise on duty, 39, 109–10
Famous Impostors, xiv
Personal Reminiscences of Henry Irving, xiv

WORKS: NOVELS
Jewel of Seven Stars, The, xiv; and archaeology, 94; influenced by Sir William Wilde, 8
Lady Athlyne, xiv
Lady of the Shroud, The, xiv
Lair of the White Worm, The, xiv; African character in, 40; and archaeology, 94; geology in, 86; racism in, 45
Man, The, xiv; as response to *The Heavenly Twins*, 58
Miss Betty, xiv
Mystery of the Sea, The, xiv; African character in, 40; racism in, 45
Shoulder of Shasta, The, xiii
Snake's Pass, The, xiii
Snowbound: The Record of a Theatrical Touring Party, xiv
Watter's Mou', The, xiii

WORKS: STORIES
"Dracula's Guest," xii, 14; rediscovered, xiv; relationship with *Dracula*, 25

Stoker, Charlotte Matilda Blake Thornley (mother), xi; mother's stories as influence, xi, xiv; response to *Dracula*, 12
Stoker, Florence Anne Lemon Balcombe (wife), xii, xiv, xv, 8
Stoker, George (brother), xi; as physician, 75

The Author

Carol A. Senf was first "bitten" by the *Dracula* bug while she was still in graduate school, and she remains fascinated by the seductive vampire count and his followers. Her other books include *The Vampire in Nineteenth-Century British Fiction* (1988) and *The Critical Response to Bram Stoker* (1993). She has also written a number of articles on Stoker and other nineteenth-century writers, including the Brontës, Sarah Grand, Charles Dickens, and George Eliot, as well as on twentieth-century popular culture. Currently an associate professor in the School of Literature, Communication, and Culture at the Georgia Institute of Technology, she received her Ph.D. in English from the State University of New York at Buffalo. She and her husband, Jay, and their two sons reside in Atlanta, Georgia.

The Editor

Robert Lecker is professor of English at McGill University in Montreal. He received his Ph.D. from York University. Professor Lecker is the author of numerous critical studies, including *On the Line* (1982), *Robert Kroetch* (1986), *An Other I* (1988), and *Making It Real: The Canonization of English-Canadian Literature* (1995). He is the editor of the critical journal *Essays on Canadian Writing* and of many collections of critical essays, most recent of which is *Canadian Canons: Essays in Literary Value* (1991). He is the founding and current general editor of Twayne's Masterwork Studies, and the editor of the Twayne World Authors Series on Canadian writers. He is also the general editor of G. K. Hall's Critical Essays on World Literature series.

THE AUTHOR

Carol Senf is associate professor in the School of Literature, Communication, and Culture at the Georgia Institute of Technology. The author of *The Vampire in Nineteenth-Century British Fiction* and *The Critical Response to Bram Stoker*, she has also written a number of articles on Stoker and other nineteenth-century writers that have appeared in *Victorian Studies, College English, Gothic,* and the *Dictionary of Literary Biography.*

RELATED AND RECENT TITLES AVAILABLE IN TWAYNE'S MASTERWORK STUDIES SERIES

The Fountainhead by Douglas Den-Uyl

The Wizard of Oz by Suzanne Rahn

The Age of Innocence by Linda Wagner-Martin

Wuthering Heights by Maggie Berg

Daisy Miller by Daniel Mark Fogel

The Portrait of a Lady by Lyall H. Powers

The Awakening by Joyce Dyer

Hard Times by Deborah A. Thomas

Go Down, Moses by Arthur F. Kinney

Les Misérables by Kathryn Grossman

Pygmalion by Charles A. Berst

Vanity Fair by Edgar F. Harden